THE AMERICAN ECONOMY

Its Problems and Prospects

THE

AMERICAN ECONOMY

Its Problems and Prospects

By

SUMNER H. SLICHTER

Harvard University

New York   *ALFRED A. KNOPF*   1950

PUBLISHED SEPTEMBER 17, 1948
SECOND PRINTING, DECEMBER 1948
THIRD PRINTING, JANUARY 1949
FOURTH PRINTING, OCTOBER 1949
FIFTH PRINTING, JULY 1950

Preface

THIS BOOK is the revision of five lectures given at the Sixth Business Conference at Stanford University in July 1947. The lectures have been substantially revised and expanded. The fifth lecture has been divided into two chapters. Figures have been brought down to date and at some points, where significant new material has become available, it has been incorporated in the text. In substance, however, these chapters are essentially the same as presented at Stanford in the summer of 1947. My wife has read the manuscript several times and has made many suggestions for its improvement.

It is one of the glories of American institutions that they give unrivaled opportunities to innovators and critics of all kinds. The large output of criticism of all aspects of American life is a healthy protection against complacency. In the field of economics it is a useful reminder that industrial institutions can still stand much improvement. It has the effect, however, of causing many Americans to underestimate the substantial merits of their economic institutions. In some respects this country undoubtedly lags behind western Europe in its economic and social arrangements, but in matters that count most it does not. The truth of this statement would be demonstrated in a sensational fashion if other countries were to remove their restrictions on emigration and if this country were to remove its restrictions on immigration. Freedom for the peoples of the world to move from one country to another would cause the United States to be deluged by a huge tide of immigration.

The present is an opportune time to examine the economic arrangements of this country. One reason why it is opportune is that a great shift of power is occurring within the United States — a shift from businessmen to representatives of employees. It is desirable that the new holders of power become familiar with the institutions for which they are gradually becoming more and more responsible. Another reason is that these arrangements are being subjected to an attack without equal in the history of the world. In the face of Russia's attempt to destroy the political and economic institutions of this country and other countries that accept the traditions of western Europe, Americans should examine carefully the merits and the shortcomings of their economy. Still another reason why a review of American economic arrangements is timely is that thinking about economic organization and policies during the last fifteen years has been unduly influenced by special conditions — the depression and the war.

One aspect of this recently developed body of thought is profound skepticism concerning the economy's capacity for expansion — a result, I think, of the proposition (called a psychological law by Keynes) that people have a tendency to save part of any increase in incomes. Overlooked is the equally important proposition that people are so eager to acquire goods that each new round of expenditures is usually a little higher than the last round of incomes. Hence expenditures and incomes have a long-run tendency to rise. Another product of depression (and perhaps of wartime) thinking is the tendency to seek solutions for economic difficulties in central planning or policy-making. In the nineteenth century the government played too small a role in economic affairs. It looks as if the twentieth century would make the opposite kind of mistake — that it would overlook the great advantages which stem from millions of centers of initiative. Still another aspect of recent economic thinking which has had unfortunate consequences for policy has been the notion that the accumulation of capital need not be encouraged. Indeed, many people think that it should be deliberately discouraged by stiff progressive taxes.

Undoubtedly the rapid growth of technological research is making the rate of industrial expansion more and more independent of public policies. Nevertheless, the prospects of the economy depend in considerable measure upon the nature of public policies. This means that they depend upon how much faith policy-makers have in the capacity of industry to grow, upon how much importance they attach to a multitude of centers of initiative, and upon how far they are willing to go in stimulating the accumulation of capital and in developing arrangements that keep the growth of production reasonably steady.

S. H. S.

Contents

THE AMERICAN ECONOMY

Its Problems and Prospects

I

The American Economy

The American economy is the most productive in
the world. With about six per cent of the world's population, and an even smaller percentage of the world's
labor force, the United States produces well over one
third of the world's goods.[1] The great strength of this

[1] Colin Clark has estimated that during the period 1925–34
the United States produced about 25 per cent of the world's income.
(*The Conditions of Economic Progress,* p. 56.) During this period
the proportion of the world's output produced by the United States
was undoubtedly less than normal and far below the postwar proportion.

One way of estimating the relative output of goods of different countries is by estimating their output of work. Mr. Thomas T.
Read has estimated the horsepower hours of work produced by
thirty countries with a total population in 1939 of approximately
1,748 million — about four fifths of the population of the globe. He
estimates that 37.7 per cent of the output of horsepower hours
produced by these thirty countries in 1939 was produced by the
United States — 1,611.9 million horsepower hours out of a total of
4,274.2 million. (*American Economic Review,* Vol. XXV, pp. 143–5.)
A considerable part of the work produced by petroleum in the
United States is used for pleasure driving rather than to make other
goods. If *all* work produced by petroleum products is eliminated

extraordinary economy is little appreciated by the people of the United States, and even less so by the people of other countries. The economy is different in important respects from economies of the past and from other principal economies of today. It has great problems, and its institutions are under attack. In fact the attack against them is the best organized and most carefully planned that has ever been launched against economic and political arrangements. It has the purpose of destroying these institutions and replacing them with very different ones.

The economy itself is undergoing a basic transformation. About fifteen years ago power began to shift rapidly from businessmen and the self-employed to employees, who are by far the most numerous group in the community. This shift of power is still in its early stages, but is going on rapidly. The prospects of the economy are much in dispute. Many people believe that it has become "mature" and that it is rapidly losing the capacity to grow. Other people think that the shift of power from employers to employees

---

from the comparisons, the United States produced 29.7 per cent of all horsepower hours.

Output of human work was calculated on the basis of 1/30 horsepower per day per capita. This method probably underestimates the production of work relative to other countries, because Americans, being better fed and better supervised than persons in many other countries, work harder and faster. This fact is offset in large measure by the fact that the work week is shorter in the United States than in other countries and a smaller proportion of the population are members of the labor force.

will undermine the spirit of enterprise and hinder the growth of industry — that no laboristic economy can be as progressive as a capitalistic one. Still other persons are impressed with the fact that industrial research is growing by leaps and bounds, and that the industrial revolution appears still to be in the early stages of its development. They count on rapid technological change to keep the economy dynamic.

The issues set forth above are the subject matter of this book. First, I shall examine the basic characteristics of the economy itself. Next, I shall explore three or four of the principal problems of the economy. Finally, I shall analyze the prospects of the economy and attempt an appraisal of its good points and its weaknesses.

I

Five principal characteristics distinguish the American economy: it is predominantly an economy of private enterprise; it is a laboristic economy — or rapidly becoming one; it is highly competitive; it is highly dynamic; and it is highly self-sufficient. Let us examine these characteristics of the economy more closely.

1. The economy is predominantly one of private enterprise. About seven eighths of the output of the United States is privately produced, and only about one eighth is produced by the government. And yet it

would be an oversimplification to describe the economy merely as one of private enterprise. Although the country has not gone far in socializing property, it has socialized a considerable part of income, and it has intervened in many ways to control the operation of markets. For example, 38 per cent of the profits of corporations (with the exception of small corporations, which pay a lower rate) go to the government, leaving only 62 per cent for the owners. A large part of personal incomes also is taken by the government — particularly of incomes above $15,000 a year. For example, even under the tax law of 1948, a married man with an income of $15,000 pays to the government about one fourth of any increase in his income. Since the personal income tax applies to returns from property as well as from personal services, the owners of stock in corporations find that any part of the profits they receive as dividends are twice taxed.

Frequently the economy is described as one of free enterprise. This is a misnomer. It is true that individuals and business concerns are left free to buy and sell and otherwise to pursue their self-interest, but it is within a framework of rules established by the government. The rules that limit the discretion of individuals and managements of business concerns are multitudinous, and their number and scope are steadily growing. Indeed, for several generations the community has been in more or less revolt against the results produced by free markets, and has been attempting to change these results by public policies.

Tariffs, social-insurance schemes, subsidies of many sorts, pure-food and drug acts, resale-price-maintenance laws, credit controls, zoning laws, minimum-wage laws, progressive income taxes, special taxes on some types of enterprise (such as chain stores), the encouragement of collective bargaining, the regulation of railroad and public-utility rates, and the regulation of the sale of securities, are all examples of this revolt.

The revolt against the market does not mean that there is not a wide area within which men are free to pursue their self-interest as they see fit, but it does mean that this area is a slowly shrinking one. Incidentally, this process of restricting the area of freedom has probably strengthened the institutions of private enterprise, because it has stopped many abuses and has made industry produce results more satisfactory to the community.

2. The American economy is a laboristic economy, or at least is rapidly becoming one. By this I mean that employees are the most influential group in the community and that the economy is run in their interest more than in the interest of any other economic group. A community composed almost entirely of employees must be expected to have its own distinctive culture — its own scales of value, its own industrial institutions, its own public policies, and its own jurisprudence. The fact that employees are supplanting businessmen as the most influential group in the community means that basic and far-reaching

7

changes are impending in the civilization of the United States.

Employees have great and growing influence, because over three out of four persons who work for a living in the United States are employees, and less than one out of four are self-employed. In addition, about fourteen million of the thirty-five million nonsupervisory and nontechnical employees in private industry are organized into trade unions. The trade-union movement in the United States is the largest and most powerful the world has ever seen.[2]

Communities composed in the main of free employees are new in the history of the world. In ancient times or in the Middle Ages the bulk of the work was done by slaves or serfs. In early modern times there grew up economies composed predominantly of self-employed. The United States was such an economy until about 1840. Only within the last hundred years have there appeared economies composed almost entirely of free employees. Even today such economies are limited to a few countries. In Russia, eastern Europe, and many other parts of the world, the workers are vassals of the state rather than citizens — they lack civil rights and are not expected to think for themselves. They are not bound to the land as were the serfs of the Middle Ages, or even to a particular industry or occupation, but they work under conditions determined by a government in which they have

[2] The so-called trade unions in Russia have a larger membership, but they are unions in name only.

8

no voice. In a rough way they may be compared to the "king's peasants" of Ptolemaic Egypt.

Evidence of the influence of employees is found in factory legislation prescribing standards to protect the safety and health of workers, in workmen's compensation legislation (applying to industrial accidents a different principle of liability from that generally prevailing), in restrictions on the terms of labor contracts in the interest of employees (maximum hours of work and minimum wages), in arrangements for compensating persons who lose their incomes because of unemployment or retirement, and, most of all, in laws encouraging employees to combine for the purpose of raising the price of their labor. Only employees and farmers who form co-operatives are permitted to combine in order to control selling prices. Any other kinds of sellers who do this commit a crime and are liable to fine or imprisonment.

Many people will deny that the United States is becoming a laboristic community. They are used to thinking of this country as the stronghold of capitalism. It is true that many other groups have great influence — especially the self-employed, who include the farmers, many small retailers, and most professional workers. It is true also that on many matters of public policy, employees have not yet had time to develop a common and distinctive point of view. Although their influence has been growing for several generations, not until the political revolution resulting from the great depression of the thirties did employees become the strongest single influence in the community. Hence it is not surprising that on many matters employees continue to accept the ideas that prevailed when employers and the self-employed dominated the country.

Some tendency to underestimate the influence of employees results from the habit of assuming that trade unions invariably are the authentic spokesmen for all workers. As a general rule this assumption is correct, but it is not always so. Especially with respect to the problem of protecting the community against strikes or lockouts in certain key industries, or with respect to safeguarding the right of employees to join unions or remain members of unions, there have been divergencies between the official position of trade unions and the preference of employees. Hence the failure of unions to control public policy on certain matters does not mean that the employee point of view is not influential.[3]

Although an increasing proportion of the workers in the United States are employees, the economy is not developing a proletariat in the sense of an oppressed and propertyless class. The view of Marx and other nineteenth-century socialists that industrial evolution would produce greater and greater poverty among workers, and greater and greater concentra-

[3] In a referendum held in Massachusetts in November 1946 on a proposal to require unions to make certain financial reports, the vote in most labor wards was overwhelmingly in favor of this requirement — though the unions strongly opposed it.

10

tion of wealth and income in the hands of employers, has turned out to be contrary to fact. Indeed, if Marx were able to visit the United States today, he would undoubtedly be amazed at the trouble enterprises have in providing adequate parking space for the "proletariat." Several observations on the failure of industrial evolution to take the course predicted by Marx are worth making.

In the first place, the gains of technological progress have not gone in the main to capitalists, as Marx thought they would, or even to consumers, but to employees. Between 1840 and 1940 the hourly earnings of nonagricultural workers increased about eightfold. The level of wholesale prices in 1940 was about 10 per cent higher than in 1840. The index of prices has an upward bias. Hence, the real price level in 1940 was moderately lower than in 1840. It is plain, however, that the principal effect of technological progress has been to raise the wages paid to employees rather than to reduce the prices paid by consumers. In spite of the steady increase in the use of capital in industry (three times as much per worker in 1940 as in 1880), the share of the national income going to property in the form of profits, interest, and rent has been declining.[4] In 1880 profits, interest, and rent were about one fourth of the national income; in 1940, about one fifth; and in 1947, about one sixth.

In the second place, technological and business

[4] The decline in the share of property in the national income could be *because* of the increase in capital per worker.

11

changes are making increased demands upon the knowledge, skill, and responsibility of the workers. This fact is in conflict with a widely held popular superstition that technological progress has been robbing workers of skill and responsibility and reducing men to automatons or robots. As a matter of fact, common labor is the one principal class of employees that is not increasing. In 1940 the number of common laborers was scarcely any greater than in 1910. Between 1910 and 1940, common laborers dropped from 36 per cent of the labor force to 25.9 per cent. On the other hand, managerial, technical, professional, and clerical jobs are increasing faster than the gainfully employed. Between 1910 and 1940 professional persons increased from 4.4 per cent of the labor force to 6.5 per cent, and clerical workers from 10.2 per cent to 17.2 per cent. Skilled workers remained a constant proportion of the labor force, and the semiskilled increased faster than the labor force. Between 1870 and 1940, technical engineers, physicists, and chemists increased from 10 to 14 times as fast as the gainfully employed; bookkeepers, cashiers, and accountants, 8 times; artists, sculptors, and art teachers, 5 times; editors and reporters, 3.75 times; musicians and teachers of music, 3 times; dentists, 3.7 times; clergymen and social and welfare workers, 1.6 times.

In the third place, a large and growing proportion of the people in the United States own property. For example, about thirty-six million people have life insurance policies, thirty million have savings accounts, twenty million own their own homes, and about nine million are stockholders in business corporations. No one knows what proportion of these property owners are employees, but since over three fifths of income payments consist of wages and salaries, a high proportion of property must have been acquired out of wages or salaries, and hence must belong to employees.

3. The American economy is highly competitive. There are, it is true, many spots where restraints are imposed upon competition. In some industries the principal competitors are so few that price cutting is discouraged, at least among these large concerns. Competition is limited also by various arrangements such as basing-point systems, patent pools, tying contracts, and contracts for maintaining resale prices. The economy would be more competitive if the new funds seeking investment each year were larger in relation to existing plant, if individuals were more willing to invest their savings in the stocks and bonds of business concerns, and if tax laws were more favorable to risky and pioneering ventures. As a result of the impediments to new investment, the vigor of competition depends largely on the willingness and ability of managements to plow back profits into the business. Fortunately, most managements have been willing to plow back a substantial part of earnings.

Despite these limits on the vigor of competition, the American economy is far more competitive than most other economies. Certainly it is more competitive than the economies of western Europe, where cartels have been either tolerated or encouraged by public policy. Likewise, it is more competitive than the economies of earlier ages, when high transportation costs protected each enterprise from the rivalry of ones in even nearby cities, when interindustry competition was less developed, when custom determined a large proportion of prices, and when the use of bargained rather than fixed prices in retailing impeded the comparison of offerings. Many people regard the economy as far too competitive — the swift pace of competition compels men to become unduly absorbed in making a living, and leaves them inadequate opportunity to enjoy the fruits of the economy.

Competition has been greatly stimulated in retailing by abandonment, in the late nineteenth century, of the practice of marking goods in code and quoting different prices to different customers, and its replacement with the practice of selling goods at prices marked on the article.[5] It has also been stimulated by the growth of chain stores, mail-order houses, and department stores. Most of these enterprises follow the policy of selling on a small margin in order to achieve a rapid turnover of goods. Not only have these large enterprises greatly increased the vigor of competition in retailing, but they have also helped to make manufacturing more competitive, because they have made

[5] Pioneers in bringing about this change were A. T. Stewart and John Wanamaker.

14

it easier for small manufacturers to get started and to grow. In 1947 there were over 27 per cent more manufacturing concerns than in 1929.

One of the most pervasive and important forms of competition in modern industry is competition between the old and the new. New houses, new automobiles, new machines, new locomotives, all compete with old ones. This year's line must be good enough and priced low enough to induce the users of the models of several years ago to discard them for the new models. Indeed, in the durable- and semidurable-goods industries the stiffest competition a producer has to meet may be from his own output of several years ago, or even of last year. Fortunately, competition in substantial measure takes the form of improving products as well as reducing costs and prices — in other words, competition relates to *both* quality and price. Economists call attempts to produce a different and better product "monopolistic" competition. This is a misleading term, because it suggests that competition is not so vigorous as it should be. As a matter of fact, "monopolistic" competition is superior to so-called "pure" competition, because it is broader and stimulates improvements in products as well as improvements in processes.

In many industries a few large concerns do most of the business, but they meet the competition of many small firms, which are ready to expand their sales whenever opportunity offers. For example, in iron and steel production (blast-furnace products), the four largest firms in 1935 did about two thirds of the business, but nearly eighty other enterprises were in competition with them; in petroleum refining, the top five concerns in 1938 owned three fifths of the assets, and presumably did about that proportion of the business, but there were nearly five hundred other petroleum refiners. In meat packing, the four largest packers made nearly half of the sales in 1939, but were faced with the competition of nearly fifteen hundred other enterprises; in tin-can production, the largest firm in 1944 did over half of the business, but had a hundred competitors; in radio manufacturing, in 1941 the four largest concerns made nearly half of the sales, but had over fifty competitors.[6]

[6] Competition between small and large enterprises in recent years has in general produced no uniform shifts in business between large concerns and small ones. The average business firm has about the same number of employees today as in 1900, but its output today is, of course, larger than in 1900. The relation between the size and the efficiency of business is in dispute. In automobile manufacturing there has been a sharp drop in the number of firms and a rise of two large enterprises to share in the business of the company that previously had made about half of the cars. In meat packing, iron and steel producing, and petroleum manufacturing, enterprises of small or intermediate size have gained at the expense of the largest two or three. A recent study of the Federal Trade Commission ("Relative Efficiency of Large, Medium-Sized and Small Business," Temporary National Economic Committee, Monograph No. 13) reaches the conclusion that large companies are generally less efficient than medium-sized organizations in terms of unit cost and rates of return.

This conclusion is disputed by John M. Blair in his article "The Relation between the Size and Efficiency of Business," *Review of Economic Statistics*, August 1942, Vol. XXIV, pp. 125-35.

The American Economy

The vigor of competition in the American economy is attributable to several conditions. The following five are especially worth noting:

a.   The receptivity of consumers to new products. In earlier economies and in some economies today, competition is discouraged by more or less fixed habits of consumption which discourage producers from seeking to attract buyers by bringing out new and different products.[7] Habits of consumption in the United States, however, are exceptionally fluid — less fixed by habit and custom than in older communities. The willingness of customers to try new goods encourages enterprises to seek to attract buyers by improving their products and by bringing out new products.

The relationship between size and efficiency varies from industry to industry. Many of the comparisons between concerns of different size are misleading, because the firms make different types of products or render different types of service. For example, a small concern may have higher unit costs than a large concern. The small enterprise, however, may specialize on small orders. If the large concern attempted to handle small orders, it would probably find that its unit costs were even higher than those of the small concern.

[7] It might be supposed that rigid habits of consumption would merely concentrate competition upon reducing costs and prices. This does not seem to be the result. Part of the explanation undoubtedly is that in a custom-bound community, custom extends to methods of production as well as to habits of consumption, and even extends to prices themselves. Part of the explanation may also be that the concentration of competition upon price tends to bring price cutting in disfavor among sellers and to build up among them mores against price cutting. Price cuts arouse such objection from one's competitors that the cuts are combined with some changes in the product itself.

17

b. The large number of enterprises — 3.8 million outside of agriculture, and 6 million in agriculture. No other economy in the Western world has a comparable number. The enormous number of enterprises is a fact of great importance, because any one of the 9.8 million concerns may be the birthplace of a new idea, the place where an innovation is started.

c. The ease with which new enterprises can be started in most lines of business. It is true that there are fields in which new concerns are not readily started, and that small and growing concerns often have difficulty in raising capital. Tax laws have added to their difficulties. Nevertheless, over 200,000 new concerns outside of agriculture are started in an average year, and for the last forty years the number of nonagricultural business concerns has been increasing faster than the population.

d. The rapid advance of science and technology. This stimulates competition because it provides industry with a large flow of new ideas, and competition in turn encourages enterprises to spend money on industrial research. I have pointed out that the number of technical engineers, physicists, and chemists has been increasing from ten to fourteen times as fast as the gainfully employed. The expenditures of business on industrial research are growing by leaps and bounds. In 1940 they were nine times as large as in 1920, and today they are more than double the expenditures of 1940. The use of science by industry will continue to grow rapidly, because the use of research by one enterprise compels its competitors to develop research.

e. The large accumulation of technological knowledge that has been built up during the last century or two. The greater the volume of knowledge, the greater are the number of materials, processes, or products to serve any purpose, and hence the greater the competition between industries. In the field of textiles, a hundred and fifty years ago consumption was largely limited to wool and linen. Cotton became cheap, and has been followed by the rayons and nylon and by the development of a variety of papers that compete with cloth at various points. Steel became cheap in the seventies, and drove iron out of many uses. More recently this field of competition has been entered by aluminum, plastics, and plywood. In power production, steam became a formidable competitor of waterpower about seventy-five years ago. More recently gasoline and Diesel engines have become competitors of steam and water power. The railroads meet increasing competition from automobiles, buses, and planes; the telegraph is having trouble holding its own against the telephone and radio. Whether one looks at raw materials, processes, or finished products, the number of alternatives is far greater today than a hundred years ago, and is constantly increasing.

4. The American economy is highly dynamic. This dynamic quality is shown partly in the rapid growth in productivity, and partly in the rapid emergence of new industries and the development of many new

products. During the last century, output per man-hour has increased at the average rate of nearly 2 per cent per year, and output per worker per year has doubled about every forty years.[8] This means that the

8 Dewhurst's estimate is 1.7 per cent per year. See *America's Needs and Resources*, pp. 22–3. There are several obvious difficulties in estimating changes in output per man-hour over long periods of time. Strictly speaking, no overall estimate is possible for the simple reason that great changes occur in what men make. Hence, estimates of changes in productivity over long periods of time ignore these changes. Estimates are reduced to physical terms by converting output in current dollars into output of dollars of given purchasing power — such as dollars of the purchasing power of 1940. This assumes that changes in the price level can be measured over long periods of time. Changes in the kind and quality of goods that are bought and sold and enter into the price indexes prevent accurate measurements of prices.

Great variation in estimates in the increase in productivity results from the use of different estimates of changes in the price level. Dewhurst derives his estimate by converting estimates of the annual income into dollars of constant purchasing power by the use of Carl Snyder's index of the general price level. Use of other indexes for wholesale prices for this purpose would have indicated a considerably larger increase in output per man-hour. The index of the general price level used by Dewhurst is probably more satisfactory than the index of wholesale prices, but neither is without its limitations.

Incidentally, the methods of estimating output per man-hour show great differences in increase from one decade to another. Decades of large increases (using Dewhurst's estimates) were 1880–90, 33.3 per cent; 1890–1900, 20.6 per cent; 1920–30, 21.2 per cent; and 1930–40, 41.5 per cent. Decades of small increases were 1860–70, 7.5 per cent; 1870–80, 3.3 per cent; and 1910–20, 7.5 per cent. There is good reason to doubt that there were in reality such large variations in the increase of physical output per man-hour. The differences between decades represent in substantial measure defects in the measurements.

standard of living of the country has roughly doubled every forty years. During the thirties, however, the increase in output per man-hour was apparently over 4 per cent per year. In 1940, output per man-hour was two and a half times as large as in 1900, and about six times as large as in 1840.[9] The emergence of new industries has been going on very rapidly — undoubtedly faster than ever before in the history of the world. The last fifty years, for example, have seen either the entire growth or the major growth of such important industries as electrical equipment, automobile, electric light and power, chemical, radio, rayon, motion picture, frozen food, airplane, and air transport. Television is just about to become an important new industry.

The dynamic character of the economy is explained in large measure by the conditions that have made it highly competitive — especially the receptivity of consumers to new products, the large number of business concerns, and the great use of industrial research. Particularly important is the large number of business concerns. As I have pointed out, every one of the 9.8 million enterprises is a place where an experiment may be authorized, where a new method may be tried out, or a new or different product may be made. No

[9] Since the quality of production greatly changed during this century, measurement of the rise in output per man-hour is not possible in a strict sense. If proper allowance could be made for the improvment in quality, the rise in productivity per man-hour between 1840 and 1940 would be even greater than sixfold.

21

regimented economy can hope to compete in dynamic drive with an economy that has 9.8 million centers of initiative.

There are, however, additional conditions that have helped make the economy dynamic. One has been the slow decline in thrift and the steady rise in the propensity to consume. Although real per capita income shortly before the war was about three times as large as in 1880, the proportion of income saved was about the same. The slow decline in thrift may have limited the accumulation of plant and equipment, but this is doubtful. It helped to sustain a high level of employment, and probably stimulated improvements in products and processes.

Another condition that has helped to make the economy dynamic has been its great capacity to produce money as well as goods. Indeed, the economy increases the supply of money far faster than it produces goods. Between 1879 and 1939, for example, bank deposits and money in circulation increased nearly twenty-five-fold, but the physical volume of production increased about 7.5-fold, and reproducible wealth outside of households almost sevenfold.[10] The

10 Physical volume of production is measured by gross national product expressed in dollars of constant purchasing power. It increased from $14.9 billion (expressed in 1944 dollars) in 1879 to $111.6 billion in 1939. (Seventy-ninth Congress, 1st Session, Senate Committee Print No. 4, *Basic Facts on Employment and Production,* p. 11.)

The estimate of reproducible wealth is that of Kuznets in his book, *National Product Since 1869,* pp. 56–228. Reproducible wealth

great capacity of the economy to produce money is important, because it means that the volume of spending
is in considerable measure independent of the volume of income — in fact, incomes are determined by
expenditures more than expenditures are determined
by incomes. Consequently if people or enterprises
wish to spend more than their incomes (a very common condition), they are not limited by the willingness of other individuals or enterprises to spend less
than their incomes — that is, by the supply of savings. The would-be spender can obtain the desired
dollars by borrowing from banks, which create the
dollars. In no earlier economies were the facilities for
increasing the amount of money so highly organized
and so efficient as today in the United States, Canada,
and some countries of western Europe. Even governments that needed to depreciate the currency in order
to pay expenses were not able to do so as effectively
as can modern economies with their highly developed
banking systems.

Technological progress, as one might expect, has
greatly increased the demand for capital, and this in
turn has produced a more or less chronic shortage of
investment-seeking funds. Many people have the impression that the economy has suffered from more or

---

comprises producers' durable equipment in both business and government; new construction, including major repairs and alterations
— residential, business, and public; net additions to the inventories
of business enterprises; and changes in net claims by individuals,
firms, and public units in this country against other countries.

less chronic oversaving. This does not seem to have
been true. Individuals have not ordinarily supplied
industry with sufficient investment-seeking funds, and
corporations have had to supplement the savings of
individuals by plowing back earnings. During the
period 1910 to 1929, for example, corporations
raised $56.6 billion of capital by issuing stocks and
bonds, but plowed back into the business $37.3 bil-
lion of profits. Even the plowed-back profits, however,
have failed to meet the demand for investment funds
during periods of expansion. Consequently the deficiency has been made up by enterprises' borrowing
from banks. Here is part of the explanation for the
enormous increase in bank deposits during the last
several generations. Of late years individuals have become very reluctant to invest in American industry.
For example, in the three nonwar years 1940, 1941,
and 1946, individuals saved a total of $44.3 billion
in the form of cash, bank accounts, securities, and real
estate, but their holdings of corporate stocks and
bonds dropped by a small amount. In 1947, a year in
which individuals purchased more private security issues than in any recent year, only $1.3 billion out of
$14.4 billion of savings of individuals in the form of
securities, deposits, insurance, and real estate was represented by the net purchases of corporate securities.

5.   The economy is highly self-sufficient. So large is
the United States, so great its variety of resources and
climates, and so efficient its industries, that in the years
immediately before the second World War less than

6 per cent of the goods and services consumed by Americans came from abroad. A hundred years ago the proportion was 10 per cent. Few countries in the world are so self-sufficient as the United States. Before the war Britain, Sweden, and Canada, for example, imported from one fifth to about one fourth of the goods they consumed, and Australia and France imported one sixth.

The fact that imports are only a small fraction of the domestic consumption does not mean, of course, that imports are unimportant. That was clearly indicated during the war when imports of rubber were cut off. Fourteen pounds of manganese are necessary to make a ton of steel. Nearly all the manganese consumed in this country comes from abroad. Without these imports the steel industry could not operate. Practically all of the nickel consumed in this country comes from abroad, and most of the bauxite used in making aluminum. Many imports, such as coffee, tea, sugar, wool, are of immediate importance in the daily lives of Americans.

II

One would not expect the American economy to be free from important and difficult problems. The very fact that the economy is highly dynamic creates the problem of maintaining stability and the problem of adjusting policies to world conditions. Furthermore, the shift of power from employers to employees creates problems. Some of the most important are more political than economic. Of the economic problems, four seem to stand out above all others in importance. They are:

1. The problem of industrial relations, that is, the problem of developing satisfactory relations between trade unions and managements, and between trade unions and the community as a whole.
2. The problem of economic stability, of keeping the economy operating steadily at high levels of employment.
3. The problem of the international economic policies of the United States, of developing policies to fit present-day world conditions.
4. The problem of incentives to expand industrial capacity and to increase production.

1. The principal problems of industrial relations are the result of the rapid rise of trade unions. During the last fifteen years the number of trade unionists in the United States has increased more than fourfold. The method of setting wages by collective bargaining in itself has profound effects upon the operation of the economy. For example, it makes the distribution of labor between occupations, industries, and places depend upon the relative bargaining power of unions and employers. The strong upward pressure of unions on wages affects the rate of technological

change, the volume of investment opportunities, the
level of prices, and the volume of employment. The
nature of the collective-bargaining process determines
the kind of community in which men live. Is collective bargaining merely a way of making *might make
right,* or is it an appeal to principle and evidence?
The answer to this question determines whether men
live in a community of power-seeking and strife or in
a community of co-operation and good will. A few
unions are able to cut off the community from essential services, such as coal, steel, electricity, or railroad
transportation. Ways of protecting the community
against interruptions of vital services remain to be
worked out. Unions must be regarded as a form of
government, because they make many rules that affect
the behavior and opportunities of both members and
nonmembers. Hence, unions raise in a new form the
problem of protecting the basic political rights of
members of the community. Unions participate with
management in making many decisions that determine the way in which plants operate and the efficiency with which goods are produced. Unions have
their own objectives, which are different from the objectives of management. One of the great problems
created by the rise of unions is that of working out
satisfactory relations between unions and management, so that unions become agents for increasing the
efficiency of industry rather than causing the productivity of industry to be impaired by a conflict for
power within every business enterprise.

27

2. The problem of economic stability is a result of the great volume of expenditures that depend largely upon men's view of the future. About one tenth of the output of the economy over the long run has gone into increasing plant and equipment, and an even larger proportion goes into replacing old plant and equipment with new. Most expenditures for expansion or replacement can be readily postponed or moved forward. When the near-term future seems uncertain or gloomy, men are reluctant to launch new ventures, and they even curtail expenditures on replacements. On the other hand, when the outlook appears to be favorable, there is a quick catching up on deferred expenditures and some expansion of new ventures. Changes in payrolls and other expenditures in the capital goods industries mean changes in the demand for consumer goods, and hence changes of employment in the consumer-goods industries. Another reason for the sensitiveness of the economy to future prospects is the credit system. This greatly helps enterprises and individuals quickly convert favorable expectations into effective demand. In addition, the short-term debts created by the credit system mean that many enterprises are quick to increase their liquidity when they expect a decline in business. Many people believe that the failure of the economy to operate steadily is its greatest fault. At any rate, something must be done to make the economy operate steadily and to assure that it will always have jobs for as many people as seek employment.

3. The problem of the international economic policies of the United States is in the main a result of the large and sudden changes that have been brought about by two world wars and a great depression, all occurring within a generation. These changes have made the traditional international economic policies of the United States badly out of date. These policies were made when the United States was trying to make headway in manufacturing in competition with more advanced industrial countries of Europe, and when it was a large debtor nation. The high tariffs that in the nineteenth century helped the United States attract men and capital, today help create a chronic shortage of dollar exchange, and thus encourage the maintenance of restrictions on trade throughout the world. The need for the United States to develop new international economic policies has been made more urgent by the great conflict over ideas between the democratic countries of the world on the one hand, and Russia and her satellites on the other. Russia is seeking to encourage the spread of communism by fostering economic chaos and distress. The United States cannot afford to stand by while Russia fosters turmoil in those countries which refuse to accept its leadership. America needs to promote political order and economic progress in all countries outside the Russian orbit.

4. The problem of incentives to expand industrial capacity and production has two aspects — a short-run and a long-run aspect. At present the prob-

lem of incentives is particularly important because the United States has a large deficiency of capital and because the military needs of the country, various governmental projects, and European aid are absorbing an unexpectedly large part of the national product. The deficiency of capital is a result of the great depression of the thirties and the war. During three years of the depression and four years of the war, plant and equipment in civilian industries were wearing out faster than they were being replaced. In several additional years the net increase in capital was very small. By 1947 employment in private industry was over 10 million larger than in 1929. As a result, capital and equipment per worker were about 9 per cent less at the end of 1947 than at the beginning of 1929.

At the same time that the United States was confronted with this large deficiency of capital, the demand for goods was running much higher than anyone anticipated. Few people, for example, predicted that the peacetime budget of the federal government after the war would exceed $25 billion. As a matter of fact, the government is spending about $40 billion a year. During the next five years the military expenditures of the country will be at least $50 billion, and they are likely to be close to $100 billion. In addition, the United States will send over $15 billion of goods abroad as part of the European and Asiatic Recovery Program. It is plain that the standard of living of the country cannot rise satisfactorily unless industry is able to increase greatly the output of goods. This means more and better plant and machines. The general public, however, as I have pointed out, shows a conspicuous reluctance to put funds into industry. The incentives for individuals to invest in American industry obviously need to be greatly strengthened.

More important than the immediate problem of incentives, however, is the long-run problem. Many people believe that the conditions that led to rapid economic progress during the last century and a half are gradually ceasing to exist, and that from now on economic progress will be much slower. Fears for the long-run future of the economy are shared by diverse groups, who give different reasons for their opinions. One group, for example, believes that investment opportunities are becoming exhausted, and that the economy is becoming "mature" and is about to stagnate. Another group believes that the institutional arrangements of modern business are becoming less favorable to progress. For example, it is asserted that the management of enterprises is falling more and more into the hands of professional administrators, who have a strong disposition to pursue cautious policies and to avoid taking risks, and that business has to be carried on within a growing framework of customs, rules, and laws that handicap the innovator and the pioneer. Taxes from now on are expected to be very high. In a society composed largely of employees,

31

taxes will rest heavily upon the well-to-do and will take a large fraction of any gain in income. The strong upward pressure of unions upon wages is likely to encroach upon profits and to limit both the funds potentially available for investment and the willingness of people to invest. Hence taxes and trade unions, it is said, will reduce the rate of capital formation and, therefore, the rate at which production and the standard of living rise.

What are the facts? Are the incentives to accumulate capital, to strive for more output, and particularly to launch risky ventures being seriously weakened? If so, should the community take steps to strengthen these incentives, and if so, what should it do?

The following four chapters will deal with the above four major problems: (1) the problem of industrial relations; (2) the problem of economic stability; (3) the problem of international economic policy; and (4) the problem of incentives to increase industrial capacity and production. This inquiry into the characteristics of the American economy and of the principal problems that confront it should not conclude, however, without an examination of the question: how good are American economic institutions? As I have indicated, these institutions are very much under attack, and they will be completely destroyed if Russia is able to do it. The shift of power from business to employees also means that the economic institutions of the community are in a state of transition. How good are these institutions? By what tests should they be appraised? How well do they meet these tests? These are the most important questions that can be asked about the American economy. In the last chapter I shall endeavor to shed light on them.

II

Co-operation or Conflict in American Industry

The trade-union movement in the United States, as I have said, is the largest and most powerful the world has ever seen. About 14 million out of 35 million nonexecutive and nontechnical employees in private industry are union members. Two thirds of the workers in manufacturing, four fifths in construction, four fifths in transportation, and four fifths in mining are organized. In the last fifteen years union membership has increased over fourfold.

The rise of trade unions, as I have pointed out, represents a profound change in the nature of the economy and confronts the community with new problems of great difficulty. The country is ill-prepared to deal with some of these problems, because it is accustomed to think of unions as weak instead of as strong. Space permits discussion of only a few of the principal problems created by the great growth of unions. I shall discuss the following six:

1. Controlling the nature of the bargaining process. Is collective bargaining bound to be a process of settling differences merely on the basis of bargaining power, on the basis of the relative willingness and ability of each side to endure a shutdown of production? Can it be developed into a process for determining what is fair — an appeal to principle and evidence?

2. Controlling the results of bargaining. Can collective bargaining be trusted to produce fair agreements in which the employers protect customers from burdensome conditions and in which the unions protect the employees from burdensome conditions? Or must the community limit the right of the parties to agree to conditions which are contrary to public policy?

3. Limiting the allowable area of industrial conflict. Shall employers and workers be permitted to jeopardize the public health, the public safety, or the economic welfare of a large part of the community in order to determine which side has the greater economic strength and is able to impose its terms on the other? Should they be permitted to injure third parties seriously in order to determine which is the stronger?

4. Protecting the rights of union members or would-be union members from undue encroachment by the union and safeguarding democratic processes within unions.

5. Developing broader and more effective co-operation between trade unions and managements in attacking problems of concern to either management or employees.

6. Preventing trade unions from causing men to attach too much attention to special interests and thereby causing the scale of values of the community to become too narrow and parochial.

I

Controlling the nature of the bargaining process is of momentous importance, because, as I have pointed out, the nature of negotiations affects both the relations between unions and employers and also the terms of the bargains.

Many people believe that collective bargaining is (and possibly *must* be) a process by which the terms of the labor contract are fixed on the basis of economic power. This kind of bargaining may produce peace, but it impedes the development of good industrial relations because it gives each side an incentive to impress the other with its toughness and its willingness to fight.[1] Parties dealing with each other

[1] It is easy to show that bargaining on the basis of power would produce peace provided neither side underestimated the other's willingness to fight. The terms on which wages and working conditions would be settled would be those which equated the willingness of the two sides to fight — that is, to endure a stoppage of

in this way could not become interested in each other's problems. If collective bargaining merely produces an armed truce or "cold" war between labor and management, effective teamwork between the two will be impossible. Settling wages and working conditions on the basis of bargaining power also prevents the terms of bargains from being affected by the public interest — by such considerations as the effect of the wage structure upon the geographical distribution of industry, and thus upon the size of the national product, and by the effect of wage changes upon prices and the general level of employment. Appeals to principle, and arguments and evidence in support of such appeals, are irrelevant when the bargain is made on the basis of economic strength. Incidentally, if collective bargaining is merely a way of settling cases on the basis of economic strength, it will not long command the respect and confidence of the community. If it loses the confidence of the community, it will sooner or later be replaced by something else.

Two steps are necessary to assure that collective bargaining is an appeal to principle and evidence, an attempt to determine what wages and working conditions are fair. The first is a widespread appreciation of why the issue is important. Otherwise the public will not insist that each side be prepared to show

---

production. Those wages and working conditions would be the best that employers would have to give and the least favorable that the men would have to accept.

good cause for resorting to lockouts or strikes rather
than continuing to negotiate or submitting deadlocks
to arbitration. The second step is the development of
a body of thought concerning what considerations are
relevant in determining the fairness of wages and
working conditions. The need for such a body of
thought can be made clear by several questions and
problems. Productivity per man-hour rises much
faster in some industries than in others. Should the
wages for a given occupation (say, machinists) rise
at the same rate in the several industries? If so, what
should be the relationship of wages to productivity?
Of what relevance are competitors' and community
wages in determining a proper rate? A union demands
a wage increase on the ground that the rates of the
employer are 15 per cent below the prevailing rate
in the community. The management rejects the demand on the ground that its rates are the highest in
the industry and 10 per cent above the rates paid by
its highest-paying competitor. Or consider the opposite case — the union demands a wage increase on
the ground that the employer is paying considerably
less than his competitors, and the employer defends
his rates on the ground that they are the highest paid
for comparable labor by any employer in the community. Does a rise in the cost of living justify wage
increases? The rise in the cost of living means that
demand is outrunning supply. Would wage increases
raise consumer purchasing power, aggravate the tend-

ency for demand to outrun supply, and thus cause the cost of living to rise more rapidly than ever?

Complete agreement on the criteria that may appropriately govern the adjustment of wages is not necessary, but there must be a well-developed and carefully reasoned body of thought upon which each side can base its arguments — a body of thought that commands respect and that neither side dare ignore. Here is an intellectual challenge of the first order — a requirement that the community on fairly short notice develop well-considered ideas on many new and complicated subjects, that it build up a body of principles reflecting the public interest, and that it insist that powerful and well-organized groups respect these principles.

II

Although the community needs to control the results of bargaining in order to control the nature of the bargaining process, the community also has a direct interest in the results of bargaining themselves. Many proponents of collective bargaining have tacitly assumed that the organization of trade unions would bring about rough equality of bargaining power between employees and employers, and that the result would be reasonably fair bargains with which the community need not concern itself. This belief is unduly optimistic. In some cases there is great disparity between the bargaining power of unions and employers; in other cases the parties may have a common interest in making agreements that are contrary to the public interest.

Three principal questions arise concerning the community's interest in the terms of bargains between unions and employers:

1. Does the wage structure produced by collective bargaining cause a bad distribution of labor and capital between occupations, industries, and places; and, if so, are the results likely to be serious?

2. Is the strong upward pressure of unions on wages likely to create problems of importance to the community?

3. Is collective bargaining likely to introduce rules into trade agreements which are detrimental to the public interest?

If collective bargaining were to fix wages in accordance with the relative bargaining power of employers and unions, and without regard to the national interest, it would prevent capital, and possibly labor, from being distributed among industries, occupations, and places so as to maximize the national product. Excessive quantities of capital, and probably of labor, would be attracted into industries in which the bargaining power of labor is relatively weak, and insufficient quantities of capital, and possibly of labor, into the industries in which the bargaining power of labor is relatively strong. Even a fairly serious maldistribution of resources between industries, occupations, and places, however, would probably

40

not substantially limit the output of industry. If the maldistribution of capital and labor were to reduce the output of about one third of the labor force by as much as one fourth (undoubtedly too large an assumption), the total output of the country (and hence its standard of living) would be cut by only 8.5 per cent.

To the loss of income from the maldistribution of capital and labor should be added the loss from "wage distortion" unemployment that would be created in those industries where the bargaining power of labor is relatively strong.[2] These industries are not likely to comprise more than one third of the labor force, and the excess work force attached to them is not likely to be more than 15 per cent greater than the number of jobs. This would indicate that less than 5 per cent of output would be lost because of "wage distortion" unemployment.[3]

[2] "Wage distortion" unemployment may be defined as the kind of unemployment that occurs when the wage rates in some plants or occupations or industries are higher than the wage rates for work of comparable skill and responsibility done under comparable working conditions in other plants, other occupations, or other industries. The rates that are relatively high attract more people than can be steadily employed. The resulting unemployment is "wage distortion" unemployment.

[3] How can one measure whether wages in occupations, plants, industries, or places are too high or too low in relation to wages in other occupations, plants, industries, or places? It is doubtful whether modern methods of job evaluation are capable of yielding satisfactory comparisons. Undoubtedly these methods will be much improved, and they may eventually become capable of yielding accurate comparisons of jobs and working conditions. No method of

that the rate of interest be high enough to compensate for the expected decline in the purchasing power of the principal. It might induce (or compel) the government and private enterprises to issue obligations payable in a fixed amount of purchasing power rather than a fixed number of dollars. Undoubtedly it would also create a strong demand that pensions and life-insurance policies be payable in purchasing power rather than a given number of dollars.

After tens of millions of people have seen collective bargaining slowly push up prices for fifteen or twenty years, and have watched the purchasing power of their savings, life insurance, and pensions slowly drop, they may demand that unions and employers formulate a national wage policy that will govern the bargains in particular industries. If such an arrangement fails to work, government wage fixing may be attempted. That would probably also lead to government price fixing. The fear of such developments might lead employers to do a better job of bargaining. Instead of granting wage increases that meant either unemployment or higher prices, employers might stand long strikes, if necessary, to avoid making concessions that could not be readily absorbed without raising prices.

Some rules in trade agreements are likely to be of concern to the community as a whole, particularly rules that compel the wasteful use of labor or prevent the introduction of new methods or materials. Such provisions reduce the standard of living of the country because they limit the output of industry. Some

44

employers, however, may prefer consenting to make-work rules and passing on the cost in whole or in part to the public rather than incurring the cost of a strike or lockout. If make-work rules become numerous, the community may be compelled to declare them to be contrary to public policy and to forbid them.[4]

III

Limiting the allowable area of industrial conflict is a problem which illustrates how ill-prepared the community is to deal with the issues created by the rise of unions. Trade union leaders and many employers (including the National Association of Manufacturers) assert that the right to strike and the right to lock out one's employees are essential parts of free and democratic institutions and must not be restricted in any way. President Green of the American Federation of Labor expressed this view when he said: "The right to strike distinguishes the free worker from the slave. The right to strike involves the foundation of our free economy." [5] The courts have attempted to limit the area of industrial conflict in various ways, particularly by limiting the right of unions or employers to injure each other. Until quite recently, to be sure, the

[4] For a well-documented discussion of this problem, see R. M. C. Littler, "The Public Interest in the Terms of Collective Bargains," *Proceedings* of the American Economic Association, 1945, pp. 209–25.

[5] *American Federationist,* July 1946.

public has been little concerned with who got hurt in industrial conflicts, and has given little support to the efforts of the courts to define the limits of allowable conflict. Within the last several years, however, the public has become more interested in protecting the rights of noncombatants in industrial disputes and especially the rights of the community as a whole.

Particularly important, of course, is protecting the community from shutdowns that jeopardize the public health, the public safety, and the general welfare. Probably never in the history of Western civilization has the community been so completely at the mercy of small groups. A prolonged and nation-wide strike or lockout in the steel industry, the coal industry, or the railroad industry would be a national calamity. Nevertheless, the community has been slow to develop ways of protecting its interests. It is plain, however, that no community can concede to any groups the *right* to imperil the public health, the public safety, or the general welfare — particularly when the groups merely desire to settle their differences with each other by a test of economic strength. Only by accident could a test of strength produce a fair result.

The ideal way to protect the country from disputes in key industries would be for the unions and employers in these industries to negotiate agreements to submit deadlocks over the terms of new contracts to arbitration. These agreements should run for a long period (say five years) and should specify the rules

46

under which arbitration would be conducted and the way in which arbitrators would be selected.

If collective bargaining fails to blanket the essential industries of the country with procedural agreements of the sort suggested, the government will probably be forced to act. A few more nation-wide shutdowns in such key industries as coal, steel, or railroads will convince the community that deadlocks in key industries must be arbitrated. As a foundation for dealing with emergencies the government should have authority to require the parties to maintain the *status quo* for a reasonable period — say thirty or sixty days. The government should have several instruments for dealing with emergencies. The first should be a "show-cause" hearing, in which the parties would be required to show cause why they should not submit their dispute to arbitration. It should be the duty of the hearing officer to endeavor to work out an acceptable formula for arbitration.

If a show-cause hearing failed to produce an agreement to arbitrate, or if such a hearing seemed inappropriate, the appointment of an emergency arbitration board would probably be desirable. Neither trade unions nor employers, however, should be given reason to expect that the emergency board might be slanted in favor of one side or the other. Hence the board should be appointed by a nonpolitical officer of the government, say the head of the conciliation service, from a standing panel of men who have been jointly recommended as neutral and competent by representatives of labor and management.

What should be done if one party or both reject the recommendations of the emergency arbitration board? It is at this point that past arrangements for handling emergencies have broken down — as is shown by the rejection by the unions of the recommendations of all major emergency boards in the railroad industry since 1941. This has thrown the disputes into the lap of the President of the United States. In some cases he has acted as a conciliator and has asked one party or the other to make additional concessions. In some cases he has acted as an arbitrator and has virtually imposed a settlement on the parties. It is obviously inappropriate for the President (or the governor) or any political officer of the government to act as a conciliator or as a self-appointed arbitrator. Likewise, government seizure of plants should be avoided — it settles nothing.

The most appropriate arrangement would be to authorize the President (or the governor) to require the parties to try out the recommendations of the emergency arbitration board for a limited period — say not less than six months or more than a year — unless they agree to different terms. This arrangement would have a double advantage. In the first place, it would introduce an unattractive uncertainty into the emergency-board procedure — an uncertainty that both employers and unions would wish to avoid. Each side would be exposed to the possibility that the President *might* require it to accept the award of the emergency board. Hence each side would have a strong inducement to settle the dispute by negotiation or voluntary arbitration. In the second place, if the parties failed to provide for a settlement of their differences, the arrangement would furnish a basis on which production would continue for a limited period. At the end of that time, of course, either party could open negotiations anew.

IV

The rules of trade unions affect the lives of their members in many ways. In three principal areas the government may need to protect union members or prospective members from arbitrary treatment: admission requirements, organizing methods, administration of discipline. With this help from the government the members of each union must themselves solve the problem of keeping its processes reasonably democratic.

The admission requirements of unions were not a matter of great public concern so long as unions covered only a small part of industry. Today there are about 7 million jobs in American industry which may be held only by persons whom unions are willing to accept as members. Obviously the admission requirements of unions are affected with a public interest. And yet over twenty unions deny membership to Negroes, seven deny membership to women, and many charge initiation fees of fifty dollars or more.

The organizing methods of unions are affected with a public interest because a few unions have used strikes, boycotts, and picketing to force men to become members — sometimes compelling them by these methods to give up membership in rival unions. Such organizing methods deprive workers of the right to be represented by organizations of their own choosing — a right protected, as far as interference by employers is concerned, by the Railway Labor Act, the Wagner Act, and the Taft-Hartley Act. Furthermore, if unions were permitted to control the membership of workers by refusing to handle the products made by nonunionists or by members of the "wrong" unions, the economy would eventually be split into two parts — one part consisting only of enterprises employing A. F. of L. workers, and buying from and selling to other concerns employing only A. F. of L. workers, and the other part consisting of enterprises employing C. I. O. workers, and buying from and selling to firms employing only C. I. O. workers.

The administration of discipline by unions is affected with a public interest because unions which have established closed shops or union shops have insisted that employers discharge workers who lose their good standing in the union. A study of eighty-one national union constitutions disclosed that fifteen unions permit members to be disciplined for "creating dissension," twenty-nine for "slandering an officer," twenty for "undermining the union or working against its interests," twenty-five for "action which is dishonorable or which undermines the labor movement." [6] Some unions permit a member who is working in a closed shop, or a union shop, and who has been ordered expelled or suspended by a union trial board, to hold his job while appealing the decision to reviewing bodies within the union. Many unions, however, require the expelled or suspended worker to give up his job in the union-controlled shop during his appeal. This appeal may take years.

The right to belong to a union, the right to choose one's union free from economic coercion by employers or other unions, and the right to remain in a union, all require protection by the government. Obviously no government can permit private organizations (1) to deprive certain classes of persons of the opportunity to work in an occupation or industry; (2) to charge stiff fees for that privilege; (3) to use the strike, the boycott, or the picket line to control men's choice of a union; or (4) to deprive men of employment because of political offenses against the union administration. New York and Massachusetts forbid unions to deny membership on account of race, color, or creed. Massachusetts, acting on the unanimous recommendation of a committee of labor, employer, and public representatives, has outlawed strikes or boycotts to compel men to change their

[6] Philip Taft, "Judicial Procedure in Trade Unions," *Quarterly Journal of Economics,* May 1945, pp. 370–85.

union affiliation, but has not outlawed refusal to handle products made by nonunion workmen. The Taft-Hartley Act goes farther — it forbids the use of economic coercion for the purpose of compelling non-unionists to join a union as well as for the purpose of compelling union members to shift one from one union to another.

Massachusetts and the national government protect the right of workers to remain in a union. In 1947 Massachusetts gave men disciplined by a union the right to hold their jobs pending appeal to higher authority within the union. It also gave union members the right to appeal from the highest authority within the union to the state Labor Relations Board, and required that if the worker were upheld by the Labor Relations Board, he be restored to good standing in the union or permitted to continue on his job as a nonmember. This means that closed-shop agreements, union-shop agreements, or maintenance-of-membership clauses are not permitted to interfere with the right of the worker to hold his job, provided the charges against him are dismissed by the state Labor Relations Board. The Taft-Hartley Act in some respects goes farther than Massachusetts, and in some respects not so far. It forbids employers from discharging men for loss of good standing in a union for any reason other than failure to pay regular union dues. It does not, however, provide a neutral source of appeal for a union member against whom charges have been made.

Many people, including many union leaders, are concerned that trade unions have not given workers broad opportunities to participate in making policies, thus giving millions of employees opportunities to lead richer and fuller lives. As I have indicated above, however, the problem of keeping unions democratic must be worked out in the main by the members themselves. The truth of the matter is that the average union member does not ordinarily wish to participate in making policies. Furthermore, he does not have the time to inform himself sufficiently about the consequences of different policies. Hence the history of trade-union government has been one of gradual shift of power and responsibility from the rank and file and unpaid officers to a full-time professional bureaucracy, and from decisions by local officers to decisions by national officers. As a union officer has well put it: "As long as things go well, the average union member doesn't want self-government and is annoyed and resentful when an attempt is made to force its responsibilities upon him. What he wants is protection and service, his money's worth for his dues." [7]

Broader participation of the members in union affairs might be achieved to a limited extent by the establishment of non-salaried national executive boards charged with the responsibility for policy making. The present boards are usually composed of full-time national officers. Nonprofessional boards would un-

[7] Will Herberg, "Bureaucracy and Democracy in Labor Unions," *Antioch Review,* Fall 1943.

doubtedly be dominated as a rule by the professional officers — just as corporation presidents often dominate the board of directors. Indeed some domination of the boards by the better-informed professionals would probably be desirable. Such boards, however, would give a few nonprofessional men of stature and wisdom an opportunity to rise to places of importance in the union, and thus would enrich the life of union members. The establishment of nonprofessional executive boards and the development of other devices for encouraging broader participation by the members in union affairs are matters that will have to be worked out in the main by each union for itself, because the arrangements that would fit the conditions in one union would not fit those in another.

V

Does the development of a large and powerful trade-union movement in the United States mean that American industry is being organized for more effective co-operation between employees and management, or does it mean that a gulf is being introduced between men and management which will prevent the attainment of the most effective teamwork in production? Trade unions can be excellent agencies of communication. They can, if they desire, help managements gain better insight into the problems and viewpoints of employees, and they can help employees learn more than they have ever known about what managements do, how they make plans and decisions, what their problems are. Trade unions, however, are intended to champion the interests of the employees. Can effective representation of employee interests be combined with co-operating with management? Trade unions also have their own leaders who may be ambitious for power and acclaim and who may prefer to pursue an aggressive and militant policy rather than to work co-operatively with managements.

In many countries of the world the rise of trade unions has tended to sharpen the differences between employees and managers. Indeed in most countries of continental Europe the labor movement accepts the belief that the essential relationship between employers and employees is conflict, and that this conflict can be eliminated only by destroying capitalism. Not only does the labor movement in many countries of Europe accept the belief in a class struggle; it fosters it and does its best to teach workers that private capitalism is a system for exploiting them and that it must be destroyed. One of the distinctive features of American civilization has been the refusal of workers to accept the idea of the class struggle.[8] Nevertheless, in most enterprises, relations between the union and the management are pretty much at arm's length — limited largely to negotiating agreements and adjusting differences. Organized co-operation between unions

[8] In a poll conducted by *Fortune* in 1939 more than two thirds of the respondents described themselves as belonging to the "middle" class. *Fortune,* February 1940, p. 24.

and management has developed in only a few plants, and no broad demand for it has developed either among managements or among union members.

The failure of union-management co-operation to develop in most plants is understandable. Managements have looked upon unions as organizations designed to limit the authority and discretion of managements. Hence the main objective of many managers has been, not to develop friendly relations with unions, but to keep the prestige and authority of management unimpaired. Union members have been deterred from developing an interest in union-management co-operation by several conditions. One is the militant tradition of the labor movement. Unions grew up as combative, power-seeking organizations. They had to fight for their existence, and only those which defeated the efforts of employers to destroy them survived. In view of these facts it is perhaps strange that American unions in general have not accepted the European idea of the class struggle.

Some union practices and policies will always be more or less of an obstacle to effective co-operation between unions and managements. It is the business of unions to be on the alert to find fault with management. This function of being management's critic, however useful to management, does not foster a demand from the rank and file that the union seek the help of management on union problems or offer to help management with its problems. Furthermore, the wage demands of unions are likely as a rule to be

quite stiff, and frequently to require that managements raise prices. Such demands do not help create
genuinely co-operative relations between the two
sides. Added to all this is the fact that the advantages
of union-management co-operation to the individual
union member, though important, are indefinite, and
are achieved only gradually and in the long run. They
consist of such things as better relations between men
and supervisors, opportunity for men to know more
about the plans of the company, opportunity for the
men to improve their working conditions by suggest-
ing changes to management, and possibly a slightly
more rapid rise in wages.

Do the conditions that have confined the development of union-management co-operation to a few
plants mean that the idea meets no real demand;
that the typical relationship between unions and managements will be an arm's-length one; and that union-
management co-operation will develop only under
exceptional conditions? In the field of industrial relations, the past may shed little light on the future.
Important changes are occurring in both managements and unions, and these changes indicate that
union-management co-operation will eventually become far more common than it is today.

In the field of management, the aloof, noncommu-
nicative, mysterious type of manager is giving way to
the administrator who feels the need of being better
informed about what is on the minds of his customers and employees, and who also feels the need of

having his own problems and, to some extent, his plans well understood by employees and customers. Typical of the new progressive executive is the head of a factory in Wisconsin who insisted that the union shop stewards meet on nongrievance matters with management once a month. He said: "I do not wish anyone around here trying to represent my employees who is not familiar with my business." The new type of management emphasizes, not the assertion of authority or the maintenance of discipline, but the wisdom and fairness of management's decisions. Executives of the new type will feel the need of co-operation from trade unions, and will often be able to get it.

Important changes are occurring also in trade unions. The militant phase of the trade-union movement, when unions had to fight for their existence, is gradually receding into the past. As unions obtain better working conditions, finding fault with management becomes a less and less satisfactory way of fostering the interest of their members. Unions feel the need for new activities. Hence some unions may welcome opportunities to work with managements to increase output, cut costs, and improve quality. By so doing, they will not become less representative of the workers — they will simply help increase the amount to be bargained over.

Experience indicates that union-management co-operative plans have a remarkable capacity to continue to function effectively even when relations between the union and management are more or less strained. The explanation seems to be that the opportunity to meet regularly with management and to offer suggestions for changes in methods of production or shop conditions is an important advantage to the union. It gives the members a good opportunity to suggest ways of eliminating heavy or disagreeable jobs and improving unsatisfactory working conditions. Once a union-management co-operative plan has become well established, it has an excellent chance of being little affected by the usual difficulties that arise between unions and managements.[9]

VI

Most important of all is the effect of trade unions upon the scale of values in the community — upon the relative importance that men attach to special interests and to general interests. Will trade unions introduce into the community a new and vigorous parochialism? Will they cause men to become more and more concerned with their special interests as carpenters, machinists, or miners, and less and less concerned with the problems of the community as a whole and their interests as members of the community? For example, will the wage demands of unions

[9] For a discussion of the effect of strained relations between men and management upon the operation of union-management co-operative plans, see S. H. Slichter, *Union Policies and Industrial Management,* pages 491–7.

increase the need for a national wage policy while unions are building up among their members strong opposition to a national wage policy? Will trade unions accentuate the need for arrangements to protect the community against the policies of certain unions, such as make-work rules or the imposition of arbitrary discipline upon members, but also intensify the opposition to such arrangements? In short, will the rise of trade unions make the country less a community with accepted common interests and make it more a collection of independent groups, each narrowly pursuing its own concerns?

Many people believe that as trade unions become more firmly established and less concerned over holding their members, they will be less completely absorbed by the short-run interests of their own members and more concerned with the problems of the rest of labor and even of the community as a whole. Trade unions, for example, might take the lead in persuading the community to adopt policies for increasing the amount of capital going into risky ventures. A stronger spirit of adventure among investors would raise the demand for labor and accelerate the advance in wages. Trade-union leaders may sooner or later discover this fact. If they do, they may regard the encouragement of enterprise as an important objective of the labor movement.

Little support for these optimistic views of the future of union policies will be found in the record of unionism. Some of the strongest and best-established unions have shown little capacity to rise above opportunism and particularism. Powerful unions have existed in the building trades for well over a generation, but no important thinking on the difficult problems of housing has originated with unions in the building industry. Few officers of these unions have taken the lead in bringing about modernization of building codes, in fostering city planning, or in sponsoring better municipal government — all needed to encourage the construction industry. Quite frequently the local leaders of the building unions (along with the local contractors) have been associated with entrenched political groups that have opposed reforms needed to stimulate building.

Equally striking is the record of the so-called operating railroad unions, composed of unusually well-informed and intelligent men who are regarded as the aristocrats of the railroad service. For many years these unions have not had to worry about survival. At a time when great changes have been needed in railroad service to help the roads hold and attract business, one might have expected unions composed of such superior workmen to be an important source of progressive ideas. As a matter of fact, these unions have largely concentrated their efforts on sponsoring new make-work laws and rules, and make-work interpretations of old rules. Thus they have retarded rather than accelerated the adaptation of railroad service to new conditions.

Perhaps one should not expect trade unions to be

much concerned with broad general interests — even the broad interests of labor as a whole. They are organized to advance the interests of small groups. Consequently the best prospect that the trade-union movement will foster interest in the problems of labor as a whole and of the entire community is through the development of strong federations that represent all of labor and view matters from the standpoint of all labor. Norway and Sweden furnish the best examples of such federations. In both Britain and the United States, however, the federations have been dominated by the member unions and rarely attempt to champion the interests of labor as a whole against the policies of the member unions. In Britain, it is true, the Labour Party has attempted to represent certain national interests (which are also the interests of all labor) against the policies of individual unions. During 1947 and 1948, for example, the Labour Party, in order to reduce Britain's unfavorable trade balance, undertook to discourage wage increases and reductions in hours and urged the desirability of a national wage policy. Eventually, the executive council of the Trade Union Congress gave assent to the government's position.[10]

The strong tradition of individualism, which is

[10] On February 4, 1948, the Labour government issued a "White Paper" entitled "Statement on Personal Incomes, Cost and Prices," in which it stated: "It is essential . . . that there be no further general increase in the level of personal incomes without at least a corresponding increase in the volume of production." The position of the Labour government was accepted by the unions.

characteristic of all branches of American life, has manifested itself in the trade-union movement in the autonomy of the national unions with respect to the federations.[11] The A. F. of L. and the C. I. O. have no more influence with the member unions than does the British Trade Union Congress. The federations are regarded as servants of the various national unions, not as their superiors. The direction of the federations is in the hands of the heads of the national unions — men who wish no interference from the federations. In the course of time the federations may cease to be merely the mouthpieces of the national unions and may become independent spokesmen for the common interests of all labor. That time does not appear to be in the foreseeable future. Nevertheless the hope that the trade-union movement will increase the importance that men attach to general interests in contrast to special interests must rest in the main upon the progress of the federations in outgrowing the domination by the national unions.

[11] It is interesting that the tradition of individualism has helped keep the national unions independent of the federations, but not the local unions independent of the nationals. In fact, strong control of the locals by the national unions is a characteristic of the American trade-union movement. The pronounced indifference of many workers to unionism, and the strong opposition of employers, created such difficulties for the unions that the locals soon learned to rely on the nationals, and the work of organizing the unorganized soon fell almost completely into the hands of the nationals.

VII

Is the community likely to do a good job of solving the great problems that have been suddenly thrust upon it by the rise of unions? That will depend upon how clearly it sees these problems, how much it cares about the state of industrial relations, and how vigorously it asserts its interests. Many people believe that the solution of labor problems is to be found solely in industrial self-government — that the development of good industrial relations is primarily the responsibility of employers and trade unions. "Encourage free collective bargaining, and industrial relations will take care of themselves," sums up this point of view.

Emphasis upon the responsibility of employers and trade unions is wholesome, but it is not enough. The community also has great responsibilities. The interest the community takes in labor matters will largely determine whether the bargaining process is an appeal to principle and evidence or merely an attempt of one side or the other to take advantage of its economic power; it will determine in large degree the effect of collective bargaining upon the wage structure, the movement of wages, and the shop rules of business concerns; it will determine the allowable area of industrial conflict, including the question whether strikes or lockouts in key industries are to be permitted to imperil the public health and public safety; it will determine whether the civil rights of union members are effectively protected within unions; it will determine, in the last analysis, whether managements and trade unions co-operate effectively to increase output and to improve working conditions; and finally, it will even determine in considerable measure the nature of the impact of trade unionism upon the scale of values of the country. Much careful thought, thorough discussion, and patient experimentation will be needed to enable the community to develop the new body of thought, the new standards of conduct, and the new concepts of fairness required to guide employees, employers, consumers, and the government in the many new situations created by the rise of trade unions.

III

The Problem of Economic Stability

Although the American economy has been growing rapidly, it has not grown steadily. During most of the last several generations, output was doubling every twenty years. In only four of the forty years between 1889 and 1929 (namely, 1894, 1904, 1908, and 1914) was the output of the economy less than in the preceding year.[1] In two of these four years, however (1894 and 1908), and in five others (1896, 1897, 1898, 1915, and 1921), the national product was well below the long-term trend — though in only two years (1894 and 1921) was it as much as 5 per cent below. If a depression be defined as a time when output is either less than in the preceding year or well below the long-term trend, there were nine years of depression between 1889 and 1929.[2]

[1] Seventy-ninth Congress, First Session, "Basic Facts in Employment and Production," *Senate Committee Print No. 4*, p. 11.

[2] Some people may object that this definition of a depression is too broad since it includes years of strong revival such as 1897

Between 1929 and 1946 the record was much less satisfactory. In twelve out of these seventeen years the gross national product was well below the long-term trend line. Indeed, after the precipitous drop between 1929 and 1933, output did not reach the long-term trend line until 1942. Failure of the gross national product to maintain the long-term trend line between 1929 and 1942 meant a loss of about $380 billion gross product in 1947 dollars, or about 26 per cent of the total output of the period.

The failure of the economy to produce steadily, as I have pointed out, is regarded by many people as its greatest shortcoming. Men are puzzled and indignant when they observe plants operating at only part capacity when millions of persons need jobs and goods. Communists believe that capitalism is inherently unstable and that depressions will eventually bring about its downfall. Some supporters of capitalism also believe that more or less severe fluctuations are inevitable, but they do not seem to realize the far-reaching consequences of such fluctuations.[3] The time is past when the community will tolerate prolonged and

---

and 1898. The definition, however, fits the essential problem — namely a less than normal level of production.

[3] The view that fluctuations of some sort are inevitable is expressed in a resolution of the International Chamber of Commerce in its meeting at Montreux in June 1947, which said, in part, "In a dynamic expanding economy, there must always be ups and downs. The objective must be to moderate, not eliminate fluctuations without stifling growth and change." The London *Economist*, June 21, 1947, Vol. CLII, p. 985.

large-scale unemployment. Unless the economy can be made to operate more steadily in the future than in the past, the community will surely experiment with radical changes in its economic institutions.

I

Why do production and employment fluctuate? Human needs do not change greatly from year to year — except when nations embark upon wars. Neither does the rate of technological discovery — although the introduction and rapid improvement of important discoveries, such as the steam locomotive or the internal combustion engine, may introduce irregularities into the rate at which production grows. At all times there is a huge volume of unsatisfied needs overhanging the market and a huge backlog of unexploited investment opportunities. With needs relatively free from short-term fluctuations, and always far in excess of productive capacity, with technological discovery going on fairly steadily, and with a large volume of unexploited investment opportunities at all times, why should not the economy always produce at capacity?

Many people believe that the business cycle is explained by a chronic tendency for supply to outrun demand. This type of explanation, however, is far from satisfactory. In the first place, a chronic tendency for supply to outrun demand would be likely to create a continuous drop in prices and possibly

68

a steady rise in unemployment rather than a series of ups and downs. In the second place, the periods that precede downturns are not periods when supply has been outrunning demand. On the contrary, they are periods when demand has been outrunning supply. Indeed, most people are usually eager to buy goods and save only a small fraction of their incomes. Many do not save at all, and a considerable number go into debt to buy goods. The explanation of downturns is to be found in the very fact that the rapid growth of demand builds up conditions that eventually cause a drop in demand.

The explanation of the business cycle should have two main parts. In the first place, it should explain why the economy is sensitive to influences tending to bring about expansion or contraction, so that an expansion or contraction, once started, tends to go on for some time. In the second place, it should explain why expansion or contraction does not go on indefinitely — why contraction soon turns into expansion, and expansion soon turns into contraction. Let us first examine briefly some of the conditions that make the economy susceptible to expansion and contraction, and then let us examine how turning points come about.

II

Several conditions explain the susceptibility of the economy to expansion and contraction. One is the high ratio of money to the current level of production. This means that a relatively small change in the disposition of people to vary the proportion of their assets held in the form of money will substantially raise or lower the current demand for goods. The ratio of money to the national product has long been increasing, and will probably continue to increase. In 1840, when the national product was approximately $1.6 billion, the total of bank deposits and money in circulation had risen to $306 million, or less than one fifth of the annual national product. By 1900, the money supply was about 65 per cent of the national product for the year, and, by 1947, about 80 per cent.[4] This means that a given rise or fall in the desire to hold money rather than nonmoney assets has four times the effect upon the current demand for goods that it would have had in 1840.

A second reason why the economy is susceptible to expansion and contraction is the great amount of spending that depends upon men's view of the future. The large expenditures of business concerns on replacements, inventories, improvements, and expansion are an example. Enterprises tend to concentrate expenditures on improvements and expansion during periods when the business outlook is bright. At these

[4] The money supply includes time deposits as well as demand deposits. If a rise in prices encouraged people to spend money more slowly, and a fall in prices encouraged them to spend it faster, the large money supply relative to incomes would be a stabilizing influence.

times growing demand creates an immediate use for new capacity, markets are most easily entered, and new customers most easily acquired. On the other hand, when the business outlook is unfavorable, enterprises endeavor to conserve their cash or to build it up by reducing expenditures on improvements and expansion and also on replacements. Much spending by consumers, especially the buying of durable consumer goods is influenced by men's view of the future. If consumers are optimistic, they increase their rate of spending and even go into debt in order to buy. That is why consumer indebtedness rises as incomes go up — such a rise is not a sign that consumers are hard up, as many people erroneously suppose, but a sign that they are optimistic. On the other hand, when incomes are decreasing and consumers view the future with alarm, they postpone buying some things and refuse, if possible, to go into debt. The dependence of spending on expectations means that expansion and contraction tend for a limited time at least to be self-sustaining or even cumulative.

A third reason why the economy is highly susceptible to expansion or contraction is the credit system. This system, as I have pointed out in Chapter I, has several remarkable characteristics. For example, it greatly increases the capacity of a rise in optimistic expectations to increase the demand for goods. Not only do more optimistic expectations cause the existing supply of money to be spent faster, but they cause spending to be increased by a rise in the total amount of money in the community. Never before has the world had such an extraordinary monetary system. Until the last century or so, people who acquired optimistic expectations were limited in their ability to increase their spending by the willingness of others to save. Today the banks stand ready to create money for 'anyone whose credit is good and who is sufficiently optimistic to be willing to borrow. Hence every time optimism becomes pervasive, the currency expands! Every war compels the government to borrow on a huge scale, and causes it to make changes in the banking and monetary system in order to facilitate borrowing by the government. Today, after the second World War, the capacity of the banks to increase credit is greater than ever.

The credit system also makes the economy sensitive to unfavorable developments. Since business concerns and consumers have at all times large amounts of short-term liabilities, an unfavorable turn in business can be embarrassing or even disastrous. Hence, whenever there is a general drop in the demand for goods, the credit system accentuates that drop. The very fact that enterprises and people have short-term debts makes them less willing to spend money, once demand begins to contract. In addition, a more or less general drop in demand causes banks and other lenders at short-term to be less willing to make new loans or to extend old ones. Hence the credit system accentuates the drop in the demand for goods by forcing debtors to use part of their incomes to pay debts

72

rather than to buy goods. In 1948, the United States is in a fortunate position, because the volume of commercial bank loans (which for the most part represent short-term debts) is small in relation to the national product — only about 20 per cent of the national product in comparison with over 40 per cent in 1929.

III

Why do not expansion and contraction go on indefinitely? Why are there frequently *changes* from expansion to contraction, and from contraction to expansion? The reasons fall into two principal groups: (1) developments within the economy which cause changes in demand; and (2) external events, such as changes in the political outlook or in international relations, which cause changes in demand. Let us analyze first how downturns occur, and then how upturns develop.

Downturns occur because demand, as I have pointed out, has a tendency to outrun supply, and, after this has been going on for several years, it builds up conditions that cause a temporary drop in demand. The eagerness of people to buy goods (evidenced, for example, by their willingness to go into debt for this purpose) needs no explanation. There are several reasons why a rapid rise in demand tends to be self-limiting, and why, therefore, demand does not long rise without interruption. One reason is that a rapid rise in demand increases prices in relation to

73

costs; a second is that it may cause some prices and costs (such as construction costs) to become too high relative to other prices; a third is that the increase in demand is financed in part by a rise in short-term debts, and thus causes short-term debts to rise relative to incomes; a fourth is that part of the increase in demand frequently takes the form of speculative accumulation of inventories.[5]

Any of the above developments tends eventually to bring about a drop in spending. For example, a rise in prices relative to costs, while immediately stimulating spending by business concerns and investors, sooner or later is likely to produce lack of confidence in the price level and to lead managements to postpone some expenditures in anticipation of lower prices.[6] If competition to complete construction work in progress pushes building costs too high relative to other prices, the starting of new projects will decline. A large rise in short-term debts relative to income is virtually certain sooner or later to cause the demand for goods to be reduced by the diversion of income to pay debts. The speculative accumulation of inventories cannot go on indefinitely; when it drops or ceases, the demand for goods declines.

[5] The rise in construction costs relative to other prices may occur because enterprises that have unfinished construction projects may bid up the prices of scarce supplies of materials and labor in order to avoid costly delays in completing the projects.

[6] In more precise terms, an abnormal spread between prices and costs arouses the expectation that at least part of the spread will be eliminated by a drop in prices.

The above explanation of downturns is to be contrasted with two widely held explanations. One is that downturns occur because the supply of investment opportunities is exhausted; the other that they occur because as incomes rise, the flow of savings becomes too large in relation to investment opportunities. As a matter of fact, the supply of investment opportunities never seems to become exhausted. Investment drops because conditions develop that make a postponement of investment desirable. As for the alleged excessive disposition to save, downturns occur while investment is being financed in a substantial measure by bank credit.[7]

Why do periods of contraction eventually turn into periods of expansion? Some of the processes that accentuate the contraction for the time being also tend to bring it to an end. For example, the urgency with which goods are offered for sale gradually diminishes. Part of the pressure to sell comes from the efforts of enterprises to reduce their short-term debts. Gradually these debts are reduced to a satisfactory level or are funded. The supply of goods is also accentuated for a limited time by the liquidation of inventories. This introduces weaknesses in prices and encourages buyers to postpone their purchases in anticipation of

[7] If downturns occurred because the supply of investment opportunities had become exhausted, or because the flow of savings was becoming too large in relation to investment opportunities, downturns would occur slowly rather than abruptly. Furthermore, as production expanded, interest rates would gradually fall rather than increase as they do.

75

lower prices. As inventories are reduced, forced selling is diminished. Likewise the drop in the demand for goods does not go on indefinitely. Distress selling may have driven prices so low relative to costs that many managers begin to expect prices to rise. Such businessmen may cease to let their inventories fall, and may even buy in anticipation of a rise in prices — thus tending to increase incomes throughout the economy. Consumers gradually get their short-term debts paid off and are able to spend a larger part of their incomes on goods. Furthermore, as personal incomes drop, the proportion of them saved also drops and the proportion spent for consumer goods rises.[8] As time passes, the need for enterprises to make repairs and replacements becomes more urgent, and the advantage to be gained from such repairs and replacements increases. Contraction in business has little or no effect upon the rate of technological discovery. Consequently, during recessions, unexploited investment opportunities accumulate. When the decline in demand shows signs of ending, the advantage in postponing the exploitation of the accumulated investment opportunities disappears.

External events are, of course, at all times affecting the state of business and may cause a change from

8 In the early stages of contraction the necessity of paying consumer debts may temporarily force an increase in the rate of individual savings. If incomes were to drop far enough, the demand in consumer goods would cease to fall, because all personal incomes would be spent for consumer goods. Rarely does contraction go this far.

expansion to contraction, or from contraction to expansion. Much of the time favorable and unfavorable events more or less offset each other, but every now and then there occurs a major political shift or an important change in international relations which overshadows other developments and which is predominantly favorable or unfavorable. The deterioration of Russian-American relations, symbolized particularly by the Communist seizure of Czechoslovakia, which led the United States to plan a large increase in its outlay on armaments, was such a development. Furthermore, the economy is not at all times equally sensitive to favorable or unfavorable events. After an extended period of expansion it becomes relatively more sensitive to unfavorable events; after an extended period of contraction, to favorable ones. A period of expansion, as I have pointed out, may cause the short-term debts of many enterprises and individuals to rise relative to their incomes, and may cause inventories to rise relative to sales, and it may bring about a drop in the backlog of postponed maintenance and of unexploited investment opportunities. A period of contraction, on the other hand, usually leads to a reduction of short-term debts and inventories relative to income, and an accumulation of maintenance and of unexploited investment opportunities. The former conditions make the economy sensitive to unfavorable developments, the latter to favorable developments. Obviously it may be difficult to determine in some cases whether an upturn or a downturn starts because of internal developments or because of outside events. Internal developments may be just beginning to produce a decrease or increase in spending when an external event adds its influence to internal changes.[9]

[9] A very complete explanation of fluctuations in production and employment should explain why fluctuations in demand do not merely produce fluctuations in prices, leaving production and employment unchanged. For fluctuations in demand to affect only prices, the demand for goods would have to be so high, relative to the physical capacity of the economy, that higher prices would not induce more output, and that a drop in demand would produce a substantial drop in prices before it affected output. It is true, of course, that additions to supply are usually obtainable only at some increase in cost to producers and in price to buyers and that, as full employment is approached, the cost of producing successive increments of output rises rapidly. Everyone is familiar with the fact that wage increases do not cause workers to insist upon a longer working day. On the contrary, wage increases often cause workers to demand a reduction in working hours. One may regard workers as "buying" income by the expenditure of time and effort. The fact that wage increases produce demands for shorter hours instead of longer hours means that their demand for income is an inelastic demand. What is true of workers is probably true of farmers, and it may be true of other economic groups. For example, a reduction in the rate of interest may stimulate saving, not discourage it — at least up to a certain point. The demand for the first two or three thousand dollars of income from investments may be an inelastic demand. Above a certain minimum, however, the demand for additional future income in terms of present income is probably elastic.

The possibility, of course, exists that a rise in demand will produce such a large and quick increase in the supply price *for each and every part of the output* (a shift in the supply curve) that no increase in output occurs even though the industry is operating below capacity. There has always been some tendency for increases in demand to produce leftward shifts in the supply curve. Now that a

IV

How can fluctuations in demand and production be limited? Two main lines of attack are possible: (1) altering the conditions that directly determine the stability of demand, and (2) developing compensatory arrangements that offset such instability as would otherwise remain.

Various developments have occurred in recent years which affect the stability of the demand for goods. The development of credit departments in banks and in business concerns and the improvement in credit-granting practices undoubtedly tend to limit the ups and downs in the demand for goods. On the other hand, the growth of consumer credit has the opposite effect, and so also may the development of term loans. Of considerable interest has been the spread of vari-

---

large proportion of wage earners are organized into trade unions, it will happen more than ever. Especially when there is a general expectation of price increases, each rise in demand is likely to produce a drop in supply and a rise in supply prices. Special mention should be made of the case of agriculture, where a drop in demand seems to *stimulate* output. The explanation is to be found in the nature of the cost of production in agriculture. The principal cost of producing most farm commodities is the labor of the farmer and his family. These costs, however, do not represent an immediate money expenditure, and they go on whether output is reduced or not. Hence only very drastic drops in price have much immediate effect upon output in most branches of agriculture. In most non-agricultural industries, enterprises have large out-of-pocket costs that vary with the size of output. Hence a drop in demand will make some of the previous output unprofitable and will force curtailment of production.

ous kinds of reports on "intentions" and "expectations," such as the "intention-to-plant reports" of the Department of Agriculture, showing the acreage that farmers intend to put into various crops; the reports on planned expenditures on plant and equipment by various branches of industry, issued by the Department of Commerce and the Securities and Exchange Commission; the reports on expected spending by consumers (and also on expected changes in personal income) issued by the Federal Reserve System; and the reports on expected car loadings and need for railroad equipment issued by various shippers' advisory boards. These reports promise to have an important influence on business and government planning and should be extended. For example, reports on the expected level of employment (or intention to increase or decrease the labor force) would be useful. Under some circumstances, reports on intentions may have an unstabilizing effect unless steps are taken to counteract it. These reports, however, improve the opportunities for both industry and government to plan for stability, and hence are an important step toward improving the stability of the economy.

Two principal steps should be taken to alter the conditions that directly determine the stability of demand. One is to give enterprises powerful incentives to make their expenditures on capital goods more steadily. The other is to limit the fluctuations of private bank credit so that changes in the volume of credit are of only limited importance as a cause for changes in the volume of spending. Let us examine these two ways of reducing the ups and downs of demand.

A powerful incentive for enterprises to make expenditures for capital goods more steadily is one of the great needs of the economy. The output of capital goods ordinarily represents over 20 per cent of the gross production of private industry. These expenditures, as I have pointed out, fluctuate widely between years of prosperity and years of depression. Between 1929 and 1932, for example, the outlay of American business on plant and equipment dropped from $11.0 billion to $2.5 billion.[10] By 1937 it had risen to $6.1 billion. Expenditures on producers' durable equipment alone dropped from $6.4 billion in 1929 to $1.8 billion in both 1932 and 1933, and rose to $5.4 billion in 1937.

About three fifths of the expenditures for capital goods are for replacement, and about two fifths for expansion.[11] The consumption of capital is far greater than expenditures on public works in time of peace.

[10] These figures do not include residential building.

[11] Kuznets estimates that from 1879 to 1938, gross capital formation in the United States was $447.4 billion, and net capital formation $187.7 billion. The difference between the two, $259.7 billion, or 58 per cent of all capital formation, represents capital consumption. The consumption of capital measures the part of all expenditures on capital goods which represented replacements. S. S. Kuznets, "Capital Formation, 1879–1938," University of Pennsylvania Bicentennial Conference, *Economics and Industrial Relations,* p. 55.

For example, at present prices capital needs to be replaced at the rate of about $11.0 billion a year, because that is the rate at which it wears out or becomes obsolete. Between 1929 and 1946 the annual rate at which capital wore out or became obsolete varied from a low of $7.0 billion in 1933 to a high of $11.9 billion in 1945. The largest expenditure on public works, however, in time of peace was $2.8 billion in 1930.[12] Hence, if enterprises could be induced to make their replacements steadily, far more would be done to stabilize the economy than could be accomplished by anticyclical expenditures on public works, provided expenditures on public works were no larger relative to national income than in the past.

Incentives for business to make replacements steadily are easily devised. A simple arrangement would be a substantial rebate in the corporate income tax to any enterprise that during the preceding five-year period spent all of its depreciation allowance for plant and equipment, and in no year of the five spent less than a given proportion of its depreciation (say 80 per cent) for plant and equipment. The possibility for the enterprise to obtain such a rebate would give managers a good reason for asking directors to authorize substantial expenditures on replacements

[12] In 1941, expenditures on publicly financed construction were $5.1 billion. Although the country was not formally at war until December 1941, most of the publicly financed construction in 1941 was for national defense and was brought about to meet the war emergency.

even in years when the business outlook was uncertain.

Expenditures on new investment are less easily influenced. The present income-tax law, however, aggravates fluctuations in new investment because it reduces the attractiveness of risky ventures relative to nonrisky ones. It discourages investments in expanding the capacity of industry in all years, but since such investments are particularly risky in years of contraction, it discourages them more in years of recession than in years of expansion. The income-tax law reduces the attractiveness of risky ventures more than less risky, because it taxes heavily the income from successful ventures but fails to permit adequate offsets for business losses. The law permits long-term capital losses, as a rule, to be offset, not against income, but against realized long-term capital gains. This is obviously an inadequate provision. The income receiver may not have any long-term capital gains, or he may not wish to realize on them, because that would require selling his interest in the very ventures that have proved most successful. Finally, the year in which he realizes capital losses may not be an advantageous one in which to take capital gains. Hence the government shares heavily in the incomes from successful ventures but very little in losses — an unfair kind of partnership and one well designed to discourage risk taking.

Two steps should be taken to correct this defect in the income-tax law. One is to permit income-tax receivers to pay a tax on their *average* income over a limited period — say five years. This would greatly improve their opportunity to offset capital losses against capital gains. A second step is to permit a substantial part of capital losses to be offset against general income in the year that capital losses are realized. The extent of such offsets should be limited — say to 50 per cent of the tax liability, or to $100,000, whichever is smaller. These reforms would reduce the tendency of the income tax to discourage new investment in periods of contraction or in years of great business uncertainty — the very times when all new ventures are most risky. Incidentally, the proposed reforms would make American industry more competitive, because they would help new enterprises to raise capital. Since investment in new concerns is, as a general rule, more risky than investment in well-established ones, an income tax that discriminates against risk taking particularly discourages investment in new enterprises.

V

The aggravation of the ups and downs of business by the expansion and contraction of credit is intolerable. The community cannot permit the volume of spending, and hence the volume of employment, to be substantially reduced by a large contraction in the volume of private credit, such as occurred between 1929 and 1933. Hence, if the community permits the amount of money to be increased by the expansion of private bank loans during a boom, it must be prepared to prevent any subsequent decrease in bank loans from substantially reducing the volume of money and the amount of spending.

The formulation of credit policy, however, must look beyond limiting the cyclical movements of credit. The credit policies of the community determine in large measure (1) the ratio of short-term bank loans to national product; (2) the supply of investment-seeking funds available to industry, and hence the capacity of industry to grow; and (3) the long-run movement of prices. Plans for the cyclical control of credit, therefore, must be only part of a much broader credit policy. This broad credit policy should have several principal objectives: (1) to keep short-term bank debts low in relation to the national product; (2) to assist industry to obtain the needed amounts of capital; and (3) to influence the long-run movement of prices. Let us examine briefly some of the problems of achieving these objectives.

1. Keeping short-term bank loans low in relation to the national product. A high ratio of short-term private debt to the national product would increase the instability of the economy, partly by making the community more fearful of a contraction of business, and hence more sensitive to unfavorable influences, and partly by making contractions more severe — since a large fraction of current income would be used to pay debts rather than to buy goods. Fortunately in 1948, short-term private bank credit is less than one

fifth of the annual net national product, in comparison with nearly 40 per cent in 1929. A good rule is that short-term bank credit should be kept below one fourth of the annual national product.

How can short-term private bank loans be kept from rising relative to the national product? The answer is simple. The total supply of money must be increased in proportion to the rise in short-term private bank loans. Then if the rate at which money is spent remains unchanged, the total volume of expenditures (and hence the value of the national product) will rise in proportion to short-term bank loans.[13] Total short-term private bank loans are now less than half as large as the total volume of demand deposits and money outside of banks. Hence an increase in short-term bank loans which produces a dollar-for-dollar growth in demand deposits will not raise the money supply in proportion to the increase in short-term private bank loans. As a result, the short-term bank loans will rise in relation to expenditures, and thus in relation to the money value of the national product — unless, as I have explained, money is spent at an increasing rate.[14]

13 Of course if the new bank deposits created as a result of the expansion of bank loans are more active than old deposits, the increase in the money supply need not be proportional to the growth in private bank loans in order to prevent bank loans from rising relative to the national product.

14 In order to illustrate this point, let us assume that physical output doubles and that private bank loans also double, rising from about $40 billion to $80 billion. The volume of demand de-

How can the money supply be increased as rapidly as the banks increase their short-term debts? There may be no problem. In the past the volume of money (bank deposits and money in circulation) has usually increased faster than bank loans. Nevertheless, this has not always been true. Between 1923 and 1929 and especially between the end of 1945 and the spring of 1948, the loans of all commercial banks increased at a faster rate than private bank deposits and currency in circulation.[15]

There are several reasons why the money supply has increased faster than bank loans. One is the production and importation of gold for monetary uses. Another is the tendency for the banks to make investments in private securities by creating deposits. A third is the large purchases of government securities by the banks — purchases made, of course, by the creation of bank deposits. In recent years government borrowing has been by far the largest source of new

posits would also increase by about $40 billion, thus raising the total volume of demand deposits and money outside of banks from $110 billion to $150 billion. This would be an increase of about 36 per cent in the volume of money. If the turnover of money remained the same, the national product would increase from about $232 billion (the present rate) to about $315 billion. The price level would drop by nearly 30 per cent. Private bank loans would increase from about 17.2 per cent to about 25.4 per cent of the gross national product.

15 Loans of all commercial banks increased from $26.1 billion on December 31, 1945, to $38.9 billion on March 31, 1948. Private deposits and currency outside of banks increased from $150.8 billion on December 31, 1945, to $164.1 billion on March 31, 1948

bank deposits, but the effect of the importation of gold has been substantial, especially since 1934.

The great need of the world for goods, and the unsettled conditions in many countries, will probably cause gold to continue to flow into the United States in moderately large amounts. Likewise, the government's budget will probably be in the red a large part of the time. Even during the last 160 years, when government expenditures were unusually low in relation to the national product, the budget showed a deficit in about two years out of five. So huge are the necessary military expenditures of the government today, and so large and many are the other demands upon the government, that deficits are likely to be as frequent in the future as in the past. In that case there will be no difficulty in keeping the national product (in terms of dollars) rising as rapidly as private bank loans.[16]

2. Assisting industry to obtain needed amounts of capital. Commercial banks have always invested to some extent in the securities of private industry. Fur-

[16] These matters are discussed more fully in Chapter V in connection with the analysis of the long-run outlook for prices.

Many people fear that a more or less steady rise in the public debt would soon saddle the community with an intolerably heavy debt burden. This would not be true if the debt were financed in a way to raise prices — unless the debt were made payable in a fixed amount of purchasing power. The rise in prices produced by deficits would be a way of repudiating debt payable in a fixed number of dollars. Hence the debt would be repudiated at about the same rate that it was incurred.

thermore, some of their loans are made for the purpose of financing purchases of equipment, or even plant, rather than providing working capital. In recent years the banks have developed the term loan to meet the needs of business for intermediate term capital. I pointed out in the first chapter that industry has been able to supply only a small part of its capital needs by selling stock to the public. Only fairly large and well-established concerns have been able to sell bonds — although today the demand from the insurance companies for bonds is greater than ever. Furthermore, most managements do not wish to incur heavy long-term indebtedness. Hence, expansion has been financed in substantial measure by plowing back earnings or by borrowing from banks and repaying the loan from earnings on the new investment. In such cases bank loans become a way of accelerating the process of expanding equipment and plant by plowing back earnings. In the future, bank credit may be needed more than ever to help industry finance additions to plant and equipment. The need of the government for money will keep taxes high, and high taxes will limit both the ability and the willingness of individuals to invest in industry.

3. Influencing the long-run movement of prices. Should the long-run objective of credit policy be to bring about a slow drop in the price level, no change, or a slow rise? A long-continued drop in the price level is undoubtedly intolerable — partly because it would increase the burden of the national debt, and

partly because, with unions pushing up money wages, a drop in prices is likely to cause severe unemployment. Hence, the choice must be between keeping the general level of prices in the long run more or less unchanged and permitting (or encouraging) a slow rise in prices over the long run.

As a matter of fact, the community may have little real choice between a stable price level and a rising one. If the budget is in the red a large part of the time, as I have suggested it will be, a rising price level will not be easily avoided. Furthermore, if unions push up money wages faster than the engineers and managers raise output per man-hour, the community will have to choose, as I pointed out in Chapter II, between (1) tolerating or encouraging an offsetting rise in prices, and (2) requiring employers and trade unions to make their wage bargains within the framework of a national wage policy. *Eventually* the community will probably attempt to keep prices from rising by adopting and enforcing a national wage policy. This result is not likely to occur, however, until the country has lived under slowly rising prices for some years and millions of people have experienced the effect of rising prices upon the purchasing power of their savings, insurance, bonds, and bond interest. One advantage of slowly rising prices in the United States would be that other countries would be helped to increase their sales to this country. This would improve economic relations between this country and the rest of the world.[17] This matter will be discussed more fully in the next chapter.

VI

Although the long-run credit policy of the government is likely to be one of encouraging a slow rise in prices, there will undoubtedly be need, during periods of business expansion, to limit the rate at which private bank credit grows. This need will be particularly great if the increase in business is accompanied by a rise in the rate at which money is spent. In some cases the problem of controlling the expansion of private bank credit may be aggravated by the fact that the federal budget is showing a deficit even at high employment.

Proposals to control the expansion of credit raise the basic question of what principles should guide the imposition of restraints on the increase in credit. In particular, what is the "right" rate at which credit should expand? The general answer to this question is that credit should increase fast enough to permit a reasonably rapid expansion of employment but no faster. Although periods of expansion are usually ac-

[17] Under present tax laws, would a rise in prices increase the revenues of the government more than it increased the expense of the government? If the answer is yes, the rise in prices would stimulate business by making possible (or at least easier) a reduction in taxes.

companied by a rise in the rate at which money is spent, some increase in credit may be necessary to permit the physical output of labor or prices to rise as fast as labor costs.[18] Since the accumulation of short-term debts, however, tends to increase the severity of the recessions that follow periods of expansion, the growth of credit should be kept down to the lowest rate that permits a satisfactory rise in employment.[19] As a practical matter, the problem confronting the makers of credit policy during periods of expansion (especially the latter phases of such periods) is likely to be how to restrain the increase in credit without inducing a drop in production and employment. The answer to this problem depends upon the instruments of control that are available, the skill with which they are used, and the timing of action by the credit au-

[18] For example, if high taxes or other conditions limit too severely the ability and willingness of individuals to save and invest, an expansion of credit may be needed (as in the past) to help finance the acquisition of plant and equipment by industry.

[19] I omit a discussion of what is a satisfactory rate of increase in employment. A rapid rise in employment which was made possible only by speculative buying of raw materials, and which was therefore temporary, would be too fast. In general, the most satisfactory rate for employment to increase is the fastest rate that does not create the conditions of a downturn.

One may question whether the best rate of credit increase should be determined solely by the effect of the growth of credit upon production and employment. If many people need to have fairly short-term credit in order to buy durable consumer goods without delay, may not a rapid increase in credit be justified by its effects upon the distribution of consumer goods? I do not believe that it would.

thorities. The object of credit policy should be to impose restraints early enough in the period of expansion so that the policy of restriction can be mild and so that it will not halt expansion itself. Two general questions are particularly important. One is whether the traditional over-all methods of limiting lending by commercial banks are an effective and practical instrument of control; the other is whether restrictions on the expansion of credit can be imposed without seriously disturbing capital markets.

1. Are the traditional over-all methods of limiting lending by commercial banks an effective and practicable instrument of credit control? These methods, as is well known, consist in the main of limiting the reserves of the commercial banks by the open market operations of the Federal Reserve banks — either by a refusal of the Reserve banks to purchase government securities at prices that are attractive to would-be sellers or by sales of government securities by the Federal Reserve banks.

It seems clear that the traditional methods of control, however useful within certain limits and under certain conditions, are not a sufficient and adequate instrument of control. They need to be supplemented. The essential difficulty arises because credit is used for a multitude of purposes and, of course, in all industries. When dangerous expansion of credit occurs, it does not begin simultaneously in all parts of the economy or in all industries. If the Reserve banks were to attempt to impose a restrictive credit policy because dangerous speculation had developed in the stock market or in commodity markets, they might halt the expansion of production and employment while millions of people were out of work. It is safe to say that the Reserve bank authorities would be unwilling to go far in applying general measures of restraint while a substantial number of persons are unemployed. On the other hand, if the bank authorities deferred imposing credit controls until full employment had been achieved, they might tolerate a large expansion of credit which made inevitable a severe contraction of production and employment.

There is no completely satisfactory escape from this dilemma. A partial solution of the problem can be achieved, however, by the use of selective credit controls. Some uses of credit are far more inflationary than others. Highly inflationary, for example, is the use of credit to finance trading in securities and commodities, the purchase of real estate or the purchase of goods by consumers. These uses of credit increase the demand for goods without increasing the supply. Among the least inflationary uses of credit are working-capital loans, because, so long as the economy is producing at less than capacity, such loans usually help to bring about an increase in the supply of goods as well as an increase in the demand for them. Of course, when working-capital loans are used to finance the speculative accumulation of inventories, they become quite inflationary. Intermediate in in-

94

flationary effect is the use of credit to finance the purchase of capital equipment. For the time being, this use of credit is inflationary because it raises the demand for consumer goods without increasing the supply of consumer goods. As soon as the new equipment is put into operation, however, the output of consumer goods rises relative to incomes.

The credit system should take account of the fact that some uses of credit are much more inflationary than others. The Federal Reserve Board (or whoever is responsible for making credit policy) should have authority to impose specific controls upon the most inflationary uses of credit. It already possesses authority to fix the margin requirements on loans made by banks, brokers, dealers, or others and secured by listed stocks. This authority should be extended to speculation in commodities. During the war the Reserve Board had authority to fix the terms of consumer credit. Such authority should be given to it again, and should be broadened to include the real-estate loans made by all commercial banks.

There is much to be said for requiring commercial banks to maintain a reserve of a hundred per cent against deposits created by the most inflationary types of loans — that is, loans to finance trading in securities and commodities, the purchase of real estate, or the purchase of consumer goods.[20] This would mean, in

[20] The hundred-per-cent reserve plan would necessitate requiring all commercial banks to be members of the Federal Reserve System.

effect, that the banks, in making these types of loans, would be acting as middlemen to put to work the savings of the community. The requirement that the commercial banks maintain a reserve of a hundred per cent against certain types of deposits would not eliminate the need for giving the Reserve Board special authority to regulate the use of credit to finance the purchase of securities, commodities, real estate, or consumer goods, but it would diminish the necessity of the Board's using this authority.

Even specific controls over the uses of certain types of credit, and perhaps the requirement that the banks maintain hundred-per-cent reserves against certain types of deposits, would not entirely eliminate the possibility of a dangerous rise in short-term debts while unemployment is still large. Hence the Reserve authorities might still have to decide whether to discourage the expansion of credit by the banks at times when there was considerable unemployment. The Reserve authorities might be expected as a general rule to risk the danger of a later collapse in order to avoid checking the increase in jobs. By the use of selective credit controls, however, the Federal Reserve System could limit particularly inflationary uses of credit without restricting the increase in employment. This would be an important step in advance. It would greatly reduce the number of cases in which Reserve authorities felt compelled to tolerate a dangerous expansion in credit in order to avoid checking a rise in employment.

The Problem of Economic Stability

2. Can the expansion of credit by the commercial banks be effectively controlled without creating grave disturbances in capital markets? This question arises because of the policy of supporting the government bond market which the Federal Reserve System adopted during the war. Its purpose, of course, was to encourage the banks and others to purchase government securities, and to help the banks increase their reserves for that purpose. As a result, the commercial banks increased their holdings of government securities more than fourfold — from $21.4 billion in December 1941 to $90.8 billion in December 1945. This enormous rise in the bank holdings of government securities gives the banks an unprecedented capacity to increase their reserves. So long as the Federal Reserve System stands ready to support the long-term government bond market at par, the commercial banks are virtually able to expand their reserves at will. Thus the responsibility for determining the amount of private bank credit in the community is transferred from the Federal Reserve System, where it belongs, to 14,000 commercial banks. And the responsibility for determining the amount of money in the community is even more dispersed than the responsibility for determining the amount of private bank credit, because support of the government-bond market means that insurance companies, individuals, corporations, and all other holders of government securities can convert them into money at any time virtually without loss.

Thus far, vivid memories of the depression in the thirties and fears that the second World War might be followed by a boom and a collapse, as was the first World War, have made individuals more willing than usual to hold large quantities of liquid assets, and have kept the banks reasonably cautious in their lending policies. It is plain, however, that the present situation is intolerable, and that ways must be worked out (1) to restore control over the total volume of private bank credit to the Federal Reserve System or some other appropriate government agency, and (2) to limit the conversion into money of government securities belonging to nonbank owners. What should be done?

Several proposals have been made. One is that commercial banks be required to hold, in addition to their regular reserves, a special reserve against deposits. It is proposed that the special reserve be composed of short-term (not long-term) government securities, cash, and, to some extent, deposits in other banks. The size of the special reserve would be determined within limits by the open-market committee of the Federal Reserve System.[21] If made large enough, the special reserve would greatly limit the ability of the banks to increase their reserves by selling gov-

[21] The proposal was made in the Annual Report of the Board of Governors of the Federal Reserve System in 1945. A good brief explanation of the proposal may be found in the *Federal Reserve Bulletin,* January 1948, pp. 14–23.

ernment securities, and it would substantially reduce the amount of credit that could be created as the result of a given increase in reserves.[22] A second proposal is that the Board of Governors of the Reserve System be authorized to require the member banks to hold higher-than-standard reserves (or an increase in standard reserves) against any rise in bank deposits after a given date.[23] The increase in reserves would reduce the ability of the banks to expand their loans, and would also reduce the attractiveness to the banks of such an increase. Still another proposal is that the support of the market for long-term government securities be continued, but that the prices of short-term government securities be permitted to move freely, and that the Federal Reserve System use open-market operations of the traditional sort in short-term government securities to control the size of the re-

[22] At the present time an increase of one dollar in reserves makes possible an increase of about six dollars in bank credit. If the special reserve were set at the maximum proposal by the Board of Governors (25 per cent of demand deposits and 10 per cent of time deposits), an increase of one dollar in reserves might permit an increase of no more than two and a half dollars in bank credit.

[23] This proposal has been made by a number of persons, among them E. A. Goldenweiser, former director of research of the Board of Governors of the Federal Reserve System, and Allan Sproul, president of the New York Federal Reserve Bank. See Goldenweiser's paper "Federal Reserve Objectives and Policies," *American Economic Review*, June 1947, p. 337, and Mr. Sproul's testimony before the Joint Senate-House Committee on the Economic Report of the President, May 12, 1948, reported in *Commercial and Financial Chronicle*, May 20, 1948, p. 30.

serves of the commercial banks.[24] Last of all is the proposal that the traditional relationship of the central bank toward government security markets be restored, and that the responsibility of the Federal Reserve System toward government securities be narrowed from support at all times to maintaining an orderly market at all times and support in periods of contraction, and that the control of the total volume of bank credit be restored as the primary objective of Federal Reserve policy.

Although the proposed special reserve would reduce the potentialities of credit expansion, and would possibly reduce incentive for banks to expand loans, it would not give the Reserve System effective instruments for checking an expansion of bank credit after the special reserve had been raised to the maximum amount authorized by law.[25] In fact, one purpose of the plan seems to be to permit the Federal Reserve System to continue the wartime policy of supporting the market for government securities. Hence the plan imposes no check on the banks' increasing their reserves and expanding credit by selling long-term gov-

[24] See, for example, E. A. Goldenweiser "Federal Reserve Objectives and Policies," *American Economic Review,* June 1947, pp. 335–6.

[25] I say that the special reserve might "possibly" reduce the incentive of the banks to expand loans because this effect is not certain. Since the banks would be required to hold considerable quantities of short-term government securities, their incentive to maintain their earnings by increasing commercial loans might be strengthened.

ernment securities or short-term securities not needed for the special reserve. Nor does the plan provide protection against the too rapid conversion of government securities into money by nonbank holders, such as insurance companies. In fact the plan in a sense encourages such conversion because it contemplates continued support of the government-bond market.

Authority for the Federal Reserve System to require larger-than-standard reserves against increases in bank deposits would be an important improvement in the country's credit arrangements. It would minimize the danger that the Federal Reserve System, in seeking to check an expansion of credit, would unintentionally produce a contraction. The proposed authority would help protect the country from a too rapid expansion of credit based upon the conversion of bank-held government securities into bank reserves, but it might not be adequate. And like the plan for special reserves, it would give inadequate protection against an increase in the money supply resulting from the sale (or redemption) of nonbank-held government securities.

The suggestion that the volume of bank reserves be controlled through open-market operations in short-term government securities, while support of the long-term securities is continued, is a step in the right direction and might prove adequate, provided the commercial banks did not hold too large quantities of long-term government securities, and provided the

101

Federal Reserve System were given authority to require more-than-normal reserves against increases in
deposits.[26] The proposal recognizes that short-term
interest rates need not necessarily be below long-
term. As a matter of history, short-term rates have
been higher than long-term about half of the time.
Any attempt on the part of the commercial banks to
increase their reserves unduly would be met by sales
of short-term securities by the Federal Reserve banks.
These sales might push the yield on short-term securities above the long-term rate. The weakness in the
proposal is that the holdings of short-term government securities by the Reserve System may not be
sufficient to check the expansion of money in the
event of a broad movement of nonbank owners to
shift from long-term government securities into better-
yielding private securities.

The possibility, therefore, must be faced that
sooner or later effective control of the volume of
money will require that support of the long-term

[26] From the standpoint of protecting the community against
dangerous expansion of credit, considerable progress has been made
during the last three years in changing the distribution of the
ownership of government securities. Between December 1945 and
March 1948 the gross debt of the federal government (including
guaranteed obligations) was reduced from $278.1 billion to $253.0
billion. The holdings of the commercial banks were reduced from
$90.8 billion to $65.4 billion. The securities due or callable after
five years or more held by the commercial banks dropped from
$27.1 billion to $10.7 billion. Hence the reduction in the debt meant
in the main a drop in the medium-term and long-term holdings of
the commercial banks.

government-bond market be abandoned, at least during periods when the demand for goods is outrunning production. Abandonment of the policy of support is not an end to be desired in itself — although much may be said in favor of permitting, or even encouraging, a rise in long-term interest rates during periods of expansion.[27] Many people believe that abandonment of the policy would cause serious difficulties for the economy. The very fact that the government has undertaken to support its long-term bonds has increased their attractiveness, and has thus helped to keep their value at or above the support price. Withdrawal of support (or a drop in the support price) would cause the prices of private securities as well as government securities to drop. Insurance companies, savings banks, and individuals, it is said, would be reluctant for the time being to purchase long-term bonds of any kind. This would hinder business concerns, states, and municipalities in raising long-term capital. The demand for capital goods would drop, and unemployment might appear in the capital-goods industries. This would produce a drop in the demand for consumer goods and a decline of employment in the consumer-goods industries. Hence the immediate effect of efforts to check the expansion of credit might be to throw the economy into recession. The drop in the price of government securities might lead to heavy

[27] Such a rise gives the banking authorities a better opportunity to combat a subsequent recession by encouraging at that time a drop in interest rates.

103

selling of these securities in anticipation of lower prices — especially selling by the banks, which are the most speculative holders of government securities, and which cannot afford to take large losses on them. The larger sales of government bonds would probably compel the Reserve banks to buy them in considerable quantities. This would increase the volume of bank reserves and of bank deposits. Hence the attempt of the Reserve banks to check the expansion of credit might eventually be self-defeating, because it might leave the commercial banks with greater lending capacity than ever, and the country with larger bank deposits than ever.

The problems that may arise from abandonment of support of the long-term government securities should not be underestimated, but neither should they be exaggerated. For example, the assumption that the abandonment of support would induce large-scale and panicky selling of government securities is open to question. The occasion for the abandonment of support would not be a period of contraction, but a period of expansion — a time when excessive optimism was leading to a dangerously rapid increase in private-security issues financed either by an expansion of bank credit or by the sale of government securities by insurance companies, individuals, and other non-bank holders. A decline of long-term government securities below par would mean that sellers at those prices would be accepting a loss that could be avoided by holding until maturity, and that buyers who held to maturity would be assured of a capital gain. Consequently long-term governments would not need to drop far below par before they became attractive relative to private issues and before the demand for them equalled supply.

This discussion of problems of credit policy has touched briefly and inadequately upon only a few major issues. It should not close, however, without mention of several matters of great moment. One is the importance of subordinating the needs of the Treasury to the needs of the country — a matter griev ously overlooked in recent years. The fact that the government is running a deficit does not mean that an easy credit policy is indicated. It may mean precisely the opposite, for the deficit may occur in periods of high employment. A second is that whatever reserve requirements are imposed should apply to all commercial banks, not merely to the banks that are members of the Federal Reserve System. A third is that the determination of government fiscal and credit policies should be largely concentrated in the hands of a Board of Fiscal and Credit Control. Congress, of course, must make appropriations and impose taxes but the Board of Fiscal and Credit Control should have general authority over the borrowing policies of the government, the management of the public debt, the basic investing and credit-granting policies of the government and its corporations, and the policies of the government with respect to the control of private credit. The fiscal and credit operations of the government are too important in their effects on the economy to be entrusted to a variety of more or less independent agencies that may work at cross purposes and with little regard to the effect of their decisions upon the economy as a whole.

VII

Although the immediate problem of credit control is one of checking expansion rather than contraction, cyclical control of credit presupposes, of course, checks on the contraction of credit as well as upon its expansion. Methods of checking contraction of credit are far less effective than control over its expansion. In periods of recession, the Federal Reserve banks have endeavored to discourage the decrease of credit by buying government securities and thus keeping the commercial banks well supplied with reserves. The policy, however, has not always been pursued with vigor and on an adequate scale. If government securities are purchased by the Reserve banks in sufficient quantities, forced contraction of credit by the commercial banks is prevented — that is, contraction induced in the case of some banks by the loss of deposits to other banks or to hoarders. Knowledge on the part of banks that they can easily obtain funds may also make the banks more disposed to renew loans or to make loans during periods of contraction.

Even if the commercial banks are not forced by the loss of reserves to contract credit, the banks may force their customers to reduce their borrowing. This action by the banks may grow out of the deterioration of the general business situation and the consequent drop in the credit standing of would-be borrowers. Keeping the banks well supplied with reserves does little to prevent the banks from becoming overcautious when the quality of risks is dropping.[28] Consequently, the contraction of credit during periods of recession must be limited in the main by support to the general business situation through government spending and through methods of encouraging business spending.

VIII

The foregoing devices for limiting the ups and downs of business will not prevent all general drops in demand. Hence the community needs arrangements to offset the fluctuations that do occur. Two principal devices are available: unemployment compensation and government fiscal policy.

Unemployment compensation is more than a method of giving relief to the unemployed. It helps sustain the demand for goods and thus to prevent unemployment. The higher the ratio of benefit payments to the wage loss from unemployment, the more effectively is this accomplished. Unemployment com-

[28] Sometimes the bankers are willing to make loans the bank examiners are not too willing to approve. No bank examiner has anything to lose by being too strict, but his reputation may suffer severely if he is not strict enough.

pensation is financed by a tax on payrolls. Hence the receipts of unemployment-compensation funds fluctuate with employment and payrolls in the covered industries. Payments from the funds vary, of course, with unemployment.[29] With proper rates of taxation and of benefit payments, the disbursements of the unemployment fund (or funds) should exceed receipts in periods of low employment. This means that incomes available for the purchase of goods are greater than they otherwise would be. In periods of high employment, on the other hand, receipts should exceed disbursements. This surplus could be useful in helping the credit and fiscal authorities control any disorderly rise in prices during periods of expansion. The surplus is used to buy bonds from the government. If there is a tendency for commercial banks to expand loans too rapidly, or for owners of government savings bonds to redeem them in large quantities in order to buy goods, the government could offset or check these tendencies by depositing in the Federal Reserve banks all or part of the proceeds from the bonds bought by the unemployment-compensation fund. On the other hand, if there is a tendency for the surplus to be too deflationary, this effect could be limited or offset by the government's de-

---

[29] Since the period under which an individual may draw benefits is limited, the cyclical movement of unemployment benefit payments is less than the cyclical changes in employment. This is particularly true in case administration of the laws is lax, with the result that unemployment benefits are paid on a large scale to people who are not unemployed but are leaving the labor market.

positing the proceeds in the commercial banks or using them to pay off government securities held by the banks or the general public.

An important advantage of unemployment compensation is that benefit payments automatically increase when business falls off. No forecasting of a recession, no legislative or administrative decisions are necessary to make it operative. Whether anyone has foreseen the recession or not, unemployment-compensation benefits are paid. The present schemes of unemployment compensation in the United States, however, have two important defects. One is that the tax on payrolls which provides the funds for the payment of benefits is based upon the employment experience of each employer in such a manner that the rate of tax is likely to be higher in years of high unemployment than in years of low unemployment. This means that as business falls off, the tax rate will rise.[30] An increase in the tax on the employers' payrolls, occurring at a time when it could not be promptly passed on in higher prices to consumers, could substantially reduce the cash balances of many enterprises and cause them drastically to reduce their purchases of commodities and services. The second

[30] The method of computing the tax liability of employers varies from state to state, but in general an increase in employment in the plant of an enterprise is regarded as good experience and entitles the employer to a reduction in the rate of taxation; and a decrease of employment is regarded as bad experience and requires an increase in the rate. There are, however, a number of complications to the method of computing the tax liability of employers.

major defect in the present unemployment compensation schemes in the United States is that they fail to provide adequate protection against the loss of wages from unemployment. Only about 74 per cent of all civilian employees in the United States work in industries, occupations, or plants covered by unemployment compensation.[31] In addition, within the covered industries only about 25 per cent of the wage loss from unemployment is offset by unemployment-benefit payments.[32] As a result of the limited coverage

[31] Government employees, agricultural employees, some employees in the processing of agricultural products, employees of nonprofit institutions, and in many states, employees in small enterprises are excluded. In a typical week in the year ending June 30, 1947, 32.0 million out of 44.4 million civilian employees were working at jobs covered by unemployment insurance — 30.4 million by the state schemes, 1.6 million by the railroad scheme. Of the 12.4 million employees not covered, 2.7 million were excluded because some state schemes do not apply to very small firms, and 8.4 million were excluded because they were employed in noncovered employments — 5.2 million in government service, 1.7 million in domestic service, 1.5 million in agriculture. About 1.3 million were not covered for miscellaneous reasons. About 12.7 million members of the labor force are not paid employees — they are self-employed or unpaid family workers.

[32] In 1946, the average benefit payment was about $18.50 per week and the average weekly wage of persons in covered industries was about $46.63. Benefits do not begin until after a waiting period of a week or more, about one out of eight workers who would otherwise draw benefits is denied benefits because he has not worked long enough in covered employments to qualify, and a considerable number exhaust their right to benefits while still unemployed. In 1946, for example, 38.2 per cent of the persons who drew benefits exhausted their right to benefits before their unemployment ceased. This proportion varied from a low of 12.1 per cent in

of unemployment compensation and the low ratio of benefit payments to wage loss from unemployment, only about one sixth of the wage loss from unemployment during the first year of a recession would be offset by unemployment-insurance benefits.

The two principal defects in the unemployment scheme of the United States are easily removed. The tax rate could be made to rise and fall with the rise and fall of employment, or rise and fall with the fall and rise of unemployment. This would involve abandoning the present practice of making the payroll tax paid by each enterprise vary directly with its employment experience. The "normal" tax rate might be 2 per cent, and might apply as long as compensable unemployment in covered industries was between 5 per cent and 7 per cent of employment in those industries. If the unemployment rate fell below 5 per cent for a period of six months, the payroll tax would rise to 3 per cent. The tax would drop to one per cent of covered payrolls if unemployment rose to more than 7 per cent of covered employment.[33] The ratio of benefit

---

Hawaii and 14.9 per cent in North Dakota to a high of 70.4 per cent in Texas and 73.8 per cent in Louisiana. Some of the persons who claimed to be unemployed after exhausting their rights to benefits had undoubtedly in fact left the labor market. No satisfactory checks have yet been worked out to determine whether persons who have entered seasonal industries for a few weeks' work are genuine seekers of employment at the end of the season.

[33] If unemployment got up to 10 per cent, the payroll tax might well be suspended and the unemployment-compensation fund might meet its obligations by borrowing. With a payroll tax as a

payments to wage loss from unemployment could be raised by extending coverage, reducing waiting periods, increasing the maximum period for which benefits may be drawn, and raising the maximum benefits that may be drawn. Since unemployment compensation helps to prevent unemployment, it is desirable to get the ratio of benefit payments as high relative to wage loss as can be done without causing large numbers of persons to prefer unemployment to work. Probably a ratio of 30 to 35 per cent is practicable provided coverage is considerably extended. Such a rise in the ratio of benefit payments to wage loss would be of substantial help in maintaining consumer demand during periods of depression.

One of the problems of operating unemployment-compensation funds arises from the possibility that the fund may run a surplus of income over disbursements during the early phase of a business contraction — thus tending to enhance the contraction. This problem would be greatly diminished in seriousness if the rates of contribution varied, as I have proposed, with the rate of unemployment.

---

credit base, the credit standing of the unemployment-compensation fund should be high. These changes could be more satisfactorily accomplished if a national system of unemployment compensation were substituted for the state systems. Good administration would be facilitated if half of the payroll tax fell on the employers and half on the employees, and if an advisory council representing labor, management, and the public were established to give advice in the administration of the scheme.

IX

The postwar expenditures of the federal government are about one fifth of all personal incomes. Immediately before the war they were less than one tenth, and in the twenties they were less than one twentieth. When government spending is so large relative to private incomes and expenditures, the entire economy is bound to be profoundly affected by whether the government is spending more or less than it is collecting.[34] A surplus in the cash budget tends to retard expansion, because it means that the government is taking more from individuals and enterprises in taxes and other receipts than it is adding to their incomes by its expenditures; a deficit in the cash budget tends to stimulate the economy, because it means that the government is adding more to individual incomes than it is taking in the form of taxes.[35]

[34] Whether the government is spending more or less than it is collecting is not necessarily shown by whether the budget shows a deficit or a surplus. Some items in the government accounts, such as the rise in the redemption value of government savings bonds, are treated as expenditures although at the time they do not represent cash outlays. Furthermore, the income and expenditures of the federal government under the old-age and survivors' annuity plan are not included in the budget. For some years to come, the receipts under the old-age and survivors' plan will exceed the deficits. Hence, the "cash budget" of the federal government may be expected to show a larger surplus or a smaller deficit than the official budget.

[35] The above statement is subject to important qualifications. The effect of deficits depends upon how they are financed, and upon the expectations they arouse. Nevertheless, the above statement is essentially true.

113

When private spending is dropping, therefore, the government should plan to collect less in taxes than it spends; in other words, to run a deficit.

How effective are deficits in the government's budget in limiting the contraction of business at a time when people are taking a gloomy view of the immediate future and when the demand for goods is dropping? There are three ways in which a deficit may be created: (1) by leaving expenditures and taxes unchanged and counting on the smaller yield of taxes to produce a deficit; (2) by reducing tax rates below the level which produced a budget surplus or balanced budget at the peak of expansion; (3) by increasing government expenditures, such as expenditures on relief or on public works. There are two ways in which deficits may be financed; (1) by borrowing from commercial banks, or (2) by borrowing the savings of individuals or corporations. The effectiveness of a deficit may be expected to vary with the way in which the deficit is created and the way in which it is financed.

Each of the three methods of creating or increasing a deficit has advantages and disadvantages. The first method of creating a deficit (leaving expenditures and taxes unchanged) creates no direct incentive for individuals or enterprises to increase their spending. No changes are made in taxes, and the government's demand for goods is not enlarged. The method does tend to halt the decrease in private spending. The drop in private spending reflects the

114

desire on the part of some people to hold more liquid assets. The deficit helps to prevent this desire from diminishing the volume of spending. It does this either by offering savers an attractive security into which to put their savings, or, if the deficit is financed by bank credit, by providing additional dollars to meet the desire for liquidity. The method may be dangerously slow. Under it a deficit develops only after private incomes have fallen, and because they have fallen. The delay in developing a deficit will be particularly serious if the budget at the height of the boom was showing a considerable surplus.

The second method (reducing taxes) may be expected to limit the drop in consumption and to help people pay their debts. Consumers will find the drop in their incomes offset in some measure by the drop in their taxes, and this in itself will make them less inclined to cut their expenditures in order to build up cash balances. Business concerns will find sales holding up better than they would have done in the absence of tax reductions. Inventories will be worked down more quickly, and the drop in profits will be limited. As a result, enterprises will be willing to spend more freely on maintenance and replacements. Temporary reductions in taxes must not be expected, however, to have much effect upon long-range investment prospects — though these prospects would be favorably influenced if enterprises could *count* on tax reductions whenever business turned down.

The timing of tax reductions is important, and it

may be impractical to make them promptly. Congress may not be in session, or there may be delay because of difficulties over who is to have his taxes reduced and by how much. A major drawback to reductions in taxes is the possibility that these reductions will create serious uncertainties concerning the future tax structure and future tax rates. When the time comes to terminate the tax cut, there may be a controversy as to whether to restore the original tax rates or to make changes in the tax structure. The possibility of controversies over whether, upon revival of business, old tax rates should be restored or new taxes should be imposed greatly limits the practical usefulness of the method of creating deficits by reducing taxes. For example, cuts as high as 50 per cent in the income tax would undoubtedly precipitate severe battles over the restoration of the old tax rates. A possible solution of this problem might be achieved by requiring the same withholdings or payments by each individual but issuing government savings bonds in return up to $1,000, or one third of the payments, whichever was larger. A substantial part of the government savings bonds would be immediately cashed, and the remainder would tend to encourage more liberal spending by their owners.

The third method of creating a deficit (raising government expenditures) has the advantage of definitely enlarging the markets for private industry. If the projects are wisely planned, they will increase not merely the immediate demand for goods, but also the volume of private investment opportunities. The method also has the advantage of giving quick results. Congress can probably be persuaded to authorize some projects in advance — to be started when unemployment reaches a certain amount. Although expenditures on projects can be made only gradually as work is done, orders for materials and parts can be promptly placed. These orders immediately affect private business. There is danger, of course, that many of the projects will be poorly selected, and will entail heavy continuing outlays by the government without doing much to increase the supply of private investment opportunities. If this happens, government spending will provoke fear of higher taxes, and the outlays on the new projects, while helping to halt the decline of business, will also limit the revival. All in all, however, the third method of creating a deficit seems to have the greatest promise. Certainly it has greater potentialities than the first method. It is less likely than the second to create controversies that offset the stimulating effect of the deficit. If projects are carefully selected so as not to increase the future tax burdens of the community, deficits created by a rise in spending can help the economy eliminate the maladjustments created by the previous boom.

Should deficits be financed by borrowing from the banks or by selling government securities to the general public? Borrowing from the banks might seem to be a far more effective method of stimulating business, because it produces an immediate increase in the money supply and also an increase in the lending capacity of the banks. The banks buy the government securities by creating deposits for the government, thus increasing the money supply. They can sell the government securities which they thus acquire to the Federal Reserve banks in order to increase their reserves.

As a matter of fact, the difference in the immediate consequences of the two methods is probably not very great, at least during periods of contraction. At such times, both individuals and institutional investors, such as insurance companies and savings banks, are in a cautious mood. They will purchase high-grade securities, such as government bonds, if they are offered.[36] In the absence of an offering of such securities, they are likely to let cash balances accumulate. The difference in the two methods makes itself felt in the main after revival in business occurs. At that time

[36] They will absorb considerable quantities of high-grade securities that may come to market through sales by previous owners. During periods of contraction, however, neither individuals nor institutional buyers are likely to purchase securities aggressively. Consequently, the immediate effect of the offering of government securities is to transfer the idle balances of some individuals and institutional buyers to the government and, through the spending of the government, to other persons in the community. In other words, the immediate effect is to increase the rate at which the existing supply of money is spent. If the government were to borrow directly from the banks, the balances of individuals, insurance companies, and savings banks would not be activated. All of this indicates that the immediate effect of financing a deficit by the sale of bonds is virtually the same as financing it by borrowing from banks.

individuals, savings banks, insurance companies, and others are more ready to purchase securities, and a larger flow of new issues is either coming to market or seeking underwriters. If the government has financed its deficit during a depression by borrowing from the banks, the revival of business finds individuals and institutional investors holding larger cash balances than they would possess had they purchased government securities during the depression. Likewise, it finds the banks holding larger quantities of government securities, and, therefore, in a better position to increase their reserves. All of these conditions are favorable for revival. Consequently, financing the government deficit by borrowing from banks stimulates revival when it comes.[37]

The method of financing the deficit should depend in part upon the long-run policy the government adopts toward prices. As I have indicated above, the volume of private short-term bank debt needs to be kept small in relation to the national income. If private bank loans rise substantially in relation to the

[37] Even if individuals and institutional buyers had purchased government securities during a depression, they might easily shift to private securities by selling their government securities. If the purchasers of the government securities were banks, the sale of government securities by individuals and others would increase the money supply. In that event, the different consequences of the two methods of financing the government deficit might be very small even during the period of revival. As a matter of fact, however, individuals and others would probably be less inclined to shift from government securities into private securities than they would from accumulated cash balances into private securities.

national income during a period of expansion, the government will need to finance the deficit in such a way as to encourage a long-run rise in prices. This would mean borrowing from banks.

X

Can a democracy such as the United States effectively pursue a policy of stability? Two basic questions arise: (1) will the community tolerate a policy of restraint during periods of expansion, and (2) are the proposed controls against deflation likely to be effective?

There is little doubt that the community can easily develop effective checks against the unhealthy expansion of business. There is much doubt, however, whether persons responsible for imposing checks will know when to apply them. There is also doubt whether the community will be willing to tolerate effective control of expansion. The experience of 1946 and 1947 vividly illustrates the difficulties of determining when to apply restraints. Throughout both years there was a very general difference of opinion among economists and businessmen as to whether the immediate problem was one of halting inflation or of averting an imminent recession. In the course of time, progress will undoubtedly be made in determining what business trends are dominant at the moment. The difficulty in answering this question, at least a large part of the time, is bound to make for indecisiveness of policy.

Inflationary policies are more popular than deflationary ones. Any proposal to discourage the most inflationary uses of bank credit — for example, such as its use in financing the purchase of consumer goods, securities, or real estate — is bound to meet formidable opposition. Helping this, that, or the other group obtain credit on easy terms is always more popular than discouraging the expansion of credit. Likewise it is unpopular to urge that wage increases be moderate. When the budget runs a surplus, no one gains votes by telling taxpayers that they must wait for a depression to receive a tax cut. Still more unpopular is raising taxes when the budget is running a surplus.

Quite different is the problem of halting contraction. Then the question is not the willingness of the community to act, but the effectiveness of the devices at the disposal of the community. A strong incentive for business concerns to make replacements steadily may be useful. Unemployment compensation helps to some extent, but it becomes effective only after contraction has gone a certain distance. Its usefulness is in limiting the depth of contraction rather than in preventing it altogether. Each of the three methods of producing a deficit has limitations to its usefulness.

These several antideflationary devices, used simultaneously, will perhaps be effective in holding contraction to narrow limits, provided the previous period of expansion did not leave the community too vulnerable to deflationary influences. Hence, the success of the community in checking contraction will depend largely upon its willingness to tolerate restraint during times of boom. If the available methods of checking deflation do not prove to be adequate, however, additional devices will have to be developed. Such additional antideflationary devices might take the form of government ownership of certain large industries, such as railroads and electric light and power (thus assuring that capital expenditures in these industries will not drop when business contracts) or special arrangements between the government and these industries to assure that their capital expenditures will be independent of business conditions.

IV

The Problem of International Economic Policy

Two world wars and a great depression, all within a generation, have brought about great changes in the productive capacity of different countries, have played havoc with world trade, and have caused revolutionary changes in methods of conducting trade. As a result, the standard of living in many countries has been greatly reduced, and the problem of restoring the prewar standard of living in many countries has been made extremely difficult. The United States has a strong interest in helping the countries that are not dominated by Russia restore their productive capacity and the flow of trade between themselves and with the United States. The traditional economic policies of this country, however, hinder the attainment of these results.

I

Each of the two great wars caused the destruction of much productive capacity in some countries, especially in Europe and parts of Asia, and also caused capital to be consumed in many countries faster than it was replaced. The long depression of the thirties retarded the rate of industrial growth and in many countries caused the consumption of capital to exceed replacements. In addition, both of the wars and the depression gave rise to economic developments and political upheavals that were unfavorable to production and enterprise. For example, many countries found their trade and revenue reduced at the very time that they were being saddled with greatly increased expenses. The resulting lack of confidence in currencies created a strong tendency to hold goods, so that domestic trade was discouraged and shortages of food and other necessities were aggravated. Furthermore, the shifts in political power caused by the wars and the depression, especially the second World War, created great doubts in many countries concerning the policies that would be pursued toward private enterprise, either in general or in particular industries. This was obviously unfavorable to the accumulation of capital. In some countries, it is true, industrial development has been greatly stimulated by the conditions produced by the two wars. By and large, however, the world as a whole has experienced few periods in the last several centuries which have been less favorable for the accumulation of capital than the period since 1914.

The two world wars and the depression produced great changes in long-established flows of trade between countries and created some new flows. The world had not fully completed the job of building a new set of trade relationships after the first World War before it became engulfed in the great depression of the thirties. The depression produced a quick crop of trade controls as one country after another attempted to protect its markets from the world-wide fall in prices. As a result, imports into Britain dropped between 1929 and 1937 from 31 per cent of the national income to less than 24 per cent; into France, from 23 per cent to 16 per cent; and into Australia, from 20 per cent to almost 13 per cent.[1]

The second World War and its aftermath have been particularly disrupting to world trade. Although the war destroyed much productive capacity in Europe and parts of Asia, it caused productive capacity in other countries to be increased, sometimes in ways that duplicated other productive capacity. Furthermore, it changed boundary lines, debtor-creditor re-

[1] Although the great depression of the thirties raised havoc with trade between countries, and trade in general was still far below the pre-depression levels at the outbreak of the second World War, recovery of industrial production from the depression was very quick and complete in many countries. Exceptions were the United States, France, Poland, and Belgium, where monetary and other public policies hampered recovery. For comparative figures see Colin Clark, *The Conditions of Economic Progress,* p. 66.

lationships, and the relationships between the price levels of different countries. It even caused substantial shifts in population — from eastern Europe to western, and from rural areas to cities. It caused the Far East to become a net importer instead of exporter of foods.

Recovery of production in Europe has been rapid — much more so than is generally realized. In the first quarter of 1948, industrial production exceeded prewar in Britain, France, Sweden, Belgium, the Netherlands, and Denmark. Only in Italy and western Germany, among the countries of western Europe, was output below prewar. The high level of industrial production, however, rested upon a precarious foundation. It was made possible by very large imports from non-European countries, particularly the United States. In 1947, imports of goods and services by western Europe from the United States exceeded their exports by $5.5 billion. Before the war western Europe had imported far more from the United States than it had exported, even including as exports services to Americans, such as expenditures of American tourists in Europe. The difference was made up by income on European investment abroad and by large sales by Europe to Asiatic and South American countries, which in turn sold rubber, tin, wool, coffee, and silk to the United States. Part of this trade, especially in rubber, tin, and silk, has greatly decreased. Within Europe the recovery of international trade has not kept pace with production.

Indeed, in 1947, trade between the countries of western Europe was little more than half of prewar. It was held back partly by the fact that the several countries could not supply each other with the kind of goods in greatest need, partly by trade restrictions, and partly by lack of confidence in the various currencies, which tended to put trade on a quasi-barter basis.

Especially serious is the problem of Britain, which has lost a large part of its overseas investments because of the second World War. Even after the first World War, Britain was still the largest creditor nation in the world. After the second World War it was the largest debtor nation. Unless the British can greatly increase their production, either to make necessary less imports or to make possible more exports, the British standard of living will be forced below the prewar level.

Fully as important as the effect of the two wars and the depression upon the conditions of production in the various economies of the world has been their revolutionary effect upon the methods of conducting trade. Before the first World War, and to a considerable extent before the depression of the thirties, tariffs were the principal restrictions upon international trade. Many tariffs, it is true, were high, and there was a strong tendency to raise them. Nevertheless, trade between countries was largely permitted to take its course, subject simply to restraints imposed by tariffs. Short-run fluctuations in exports or im-

127

ports were not regarded as calling for any action except possibly changes in discount rates of central banks. The policy of noninterference worked because cost levels, price levels, patterns of production, debtor-creditor relationships, and capital flows were all more or less adjusted to one another.

Today nearly all countries of the world except the United States place comprehensive and highly detailed controls upon international trade. These controls take various forms — government purchasing plans, government sales plans, bilateral trading agreements, controls of foreign exchange, and the licensing of exports and imports. They are the inevitable results of huge accumulated needs, impaired power to produce, unstable currencies, and limited reserves of foreign exchange — all created by the war. Countries faced with acute shortages must obviously place first things first. They must require that foreign exchange be used for necessities before luxuries, and that the national interest determine how much foreign exchange shall be used to buy consumer goods and how much to buy capital goods.

Necessary as the new methods of conducting trade may be during the period immediately following the war, they have important disadvantages. In the first place, they have a strong tendency to perpetuate bilateral arrangements — an arrangement for country A to take certain quantities of products from country B in return for country B's agreeing to take certain products from country A. Such arrangements prevent the best use of resources because trade is not naturally bilateral. If country A has a surplus that country B could use, it would be only accidental that country B would have a surplus that country A could use. In short, bilateralism has the same disadvantages in trade between countries as does barter in trade between individuals. In the second place, the new methods of trading are unfavorable to the long-run growth of commerce because an increase in imports is not trusted to produce an early rise in exports. Hence, unless new opportunities to export are seen, or unless the imports of one commodity will reduce the imports of another, a given importation may not be permitted. As a result, the opportunity of industry to experiment in developing new markets or in using new materials is restricted, and the economies of the world are less able to be dynamic, to hunt for new markets in any part of the world, and to trade wherever trading may be advantageous. Finally, the new methods of trading are likely to have unfortunate political consequences. They tie various countries together to the exclusion of other countries, create undue dependence of some countries upon others, and foster rivalries and misunderstandings between countries that are parties to bilateral arrangements and countries that are not.

II

What is the stake of the United States in restoring production disrupted by the war and postwar disturbances, and in developing lasting arrangements that are favorable to trade between countries?

To begin with, the United States has a direct economic interest in fostering production in other countries and trade with them because this country needs more imports. For over a generation the United States has been severely handicapped in exporting part of the output of its most efficient industries by the difficulties of other countries in selling to the United States. More imports would help this country gain full advantage of the exceptional superiority of some of its industries — particularly the automobile industry, the electrical-equipment industry, and the machinery-producing industries in general. If other countries were able to make larger sales to the United States, this country would be able to export larger quantities of the products of the industries where labor and capital are especially efficient. The more effective use of labor and resources would mean more output per man-hour and a higher standard of living for Americans in general.

Even more important than the economic interests of the United States in restoring production in other countries and in rebuilding trade between them are its political interests. These political interests spring from the great ideological conflict between Russia and her satellites on the one hand, and the democratic and liberal states on the other. The attempt of Russia to impose communism on the world has created one of the great conflicts of all time, and it is the most important fact about the world today.

At all times, of course, there have been governments that have attempted to regiment the people and to deny them participation in policy making. Most dictatorships of the past, however, have permitted communication between their people and the rest of the world, and have allowed individuals considerable latitude in selecting their own activities and in planning their lives. The dictatorship of Russia is unique in the completeness with which it shuts off its people from the rest of the world and requires the acceptance of the official point of view. Furthermore, it is unique in the aggressiveness with which it attacks the institutions of other countries and endeavors to destroy free and democratic institutions wherever they exist.

During most of the last several centuries the aggressors in the conflict between dictatorships and the democratic or liberal philosophy have been the proponents of democracy. They have endeavored to spread the idea of civil rights and to gain acceptance for the principle that public policies should be made with broad participation by members of the community. During most of this time the absolute monarchies or police states have been on the defensive. Today the situation is different. The police states, headed by

Russia, are on the march, and the democracies are on the defensive. Democracy, for the time being, has lost the evangelical spirit, the will, and possibly the ability to spread its ideas through the world. Furthermore, the proponents of dictatorships have changed the basis of their appeal. Just as the old absolute monarchs claimed to rule by divine right, the Russian dictatorship claims to possess a mandate from the masses. It appropriates the vocabulary of the democratic movement and claims to be the only true exponent of democracy.

It is the great ideological battle between the police states and the democracies which gives the United States such a strong interest in the prosperity and economic progress of other countries — especially the democratic countries. Policies designed to encourage prosperity in other countries, of course, cannot alone be expected to prevent the spread of communism. They will not prevent Communists from seizing control of trade unions, from giving military supplies to guerrilla bands, from developing highly disciplined and well-armed groups ready to seize the government. Prosperity and progress do not assure that people will accept and cherish the democratic philosophy — particularly if their traditions have not been democratic. Misery and despair, however, are the best allies that communism has in its efforts to dominate the world. That is why Communists attempt to disrupt the economic life of countries they would take over. That is why a necessary *part* of the policy of the United States against communism should be to foster prosperity and progress in other countries — though the people of the United States should bear in mind that the very success of this country in fostering prosperity will cause the Communists to redouble their efforts to seize control of foreign labor movements and to plan for the seizure of governments by organized minorities.

Finally, the political interest of the United States in restoring production in other countries and trade between countries gives rise to a special economic interest. The net cost to this country in helping other countries can be either very great or quite small, depending upon whether or not they can pay for most of what they receive. They can pay only by selling directly or indirectly to the United States. Larger imports in return for the goods sent abroad by the United States to help other countries mean a higher standard of living for Americans. Rich and productive as this country is, it cannot afford to overlook the effect upon its standard of living of a few billion dollars additional each year in the form of imports.

III

How can the United States help to foster prosperity in other countries and to restore conditions that would be favorable to the growth of international trade? The United States has already done much to help to restore production and trade throughout the world. It has played a leading role in establishing the International Bank for Reconstruction and Development and the International Monetary Fund. The former is designed to help countries obtain capital, and the latter, to promote stable rates of exchange — particularly to protect exchange rates against short-term fluctuations. The United States is by far the largest contributor to the capital of both the bank and the fund. It has also taken the lead in sponsoring the establishment of the International Trade Organization. This is an organization of nearly sixty countries representing over ninety per cent of prewar world trade. These countries have become parties to a charter pledging themselves to encourage trade by eliminating discrimination in international commerce and by reducing tariffs and other barriers to commerce. The charter contains many loopholes and ambiguities, but it commits the members in principle to promoting freer trade. Through the reciprocal trade agreement program sponsored by Secretary Hull, the United States prior to 1945 had made agreements with twenty-nine countries substantially reducing duties on a large part of its imports. At Geneva in 1947 the United States participated in an epoch-making conference at which representatives of twenty-three countries, including the United States, negotiated 45,000 separate tariff concessions on products that represented almost half of the world's imports in 1938. The loans, gifts, grants, and relief by the United States and its citizens to the countries of western and southern Europe and

Turkey between July 1, 1945, and December 31, 1947, were over $11 billion. In addition, considerable aid was given to countries in Asia. Under the European and Asiatic Recovery Program (the so-called "Marshall Plan") the United States in the next four years will probably contribute at least $16 billion to the relief and rehabilitation of various countries in western and southern Europe and in Asia.

The contributions the United States has made to the restoration of production and trade throughout the world, in the form of tariff concessions, contributions to the capital of international financial institutions, and gifts and loans to other countries, far transcend the efforts any country has ever made to help other countries increase their production and trade. And yet it is doubtful whether even the help the United States has given and is about to give under the European and Asiatic Recovery Program will be sufficient to meet the needs of the other countries and the interest of the United States in expanding world trade.

The European Recovery Program contemplates, it is true, substantial additions to the productive capacity of western and southern Europe. By the end of 1951, crude-steel production, for example, is intended to be about 20 per cent above prewar; oil-refining capacity two and one half times prewar; the output of electricity two thirds above prewar. These and other production goals may not be easily attained. For several decades Europe has not provided a particu-

135

larly favorable environment for enterprise. Some important European countries have not realized the great need for encouraging the accumulation of capital and the replacement of old plant and equipment with new, or fostering vigorous competition among businessmen. A large part of the wage earners in Europe are committed to the belief that the essential relationship between employees and private employers is warfare. These wage earners are part of a well-organized movement to replace private industry with public. Private enterprise cannot be expected to flourish in countries where there is a vigorous drive to destroy it. The Russians and their powerful co-workers in various European countries will do their best to defeat the efforts of the United States to help the countries of Europe build up production.

Even if the production goals contemplated by the European and Asiatic Recovery Program are realized and surpassed, the problem of restoring a healthy world economy will not necessarily have been achieved. The crucial question is whether the increase in productive capacity enables the countries participating in the recovery program to pay for their imports. Both the European experts of the Committee of European Economic Co-operation and the American experts who have reviewed the program estimate that the exports of the countries participating in the European Recovery Program will not be large enough by 1951 to pay for their imports. The European experts put the export deficiency of the countries participating in the Marshall Plan (including western Germany) at $1.6 billion in 1951.[2] The American experts assume that the deficiency in exports of the participating countries will range from $1.7 billion to $3.3 billion in the year from July 1, 1951, to June 30, 1952.[3]

These conclusions are obviously highly important, and also highly disturbing. If the participating countries cannot pay for their imports, either the United States (or some other country) will have to continue to give them aid by gifts or loans, or the participating countries will have to cut their imports. Cutting imports would not necessarily mean a reduction in the immediate standard of living of the participating countries, because the reduction in imports might be limited to capital goods. Hence the reduction might retard the rate at which countries raised their standard of living, rather than force them to make an immediate reduction in consumption. Nevertheless, some reduction in consumption would not be easily avoided; if it occurred, it would mean a lower standard of living, and would probably produce great un-

[2] Committee of European Economic Co-operation, *General Report*, Vol. I, p. 113. These estimates assume an important change in the terms of trade in favor of the European countries. It is as sumed that exports from Europe in 1951 will be made at prices ruling on the first of July 1947. For imports, however, it is assumed that there will be a reduction in prices, as compared with July 1, 1947, of 7.5 per cent in 1949, 10 per cent in 1950, and 12½ per cent in 1951.

[3] 80th Congress, First Session, Senate Committee on Foreign Relations, *Outline of European Recovery Program*, p. 111.

rest. Furthermore, if paying for imports remains a problem for many countries, they are bound to maintain restrictions on trade, and to be unwilling to adopt many methods of trading that are favorable to the expansion of commerce between countries. The International Trade Organization Charter would not effectively prevent the enforcement of restrictions on trade. Finally, difficulties in paying for imports will create ill will toward the United States, because borrowing countries will have trouble in paying interest on their loans. This would weaken the influence of the United States throughout the world.

Why are many countries likely to have trouble even as late as 1951 in exporting enough to pay for their imports? The crux of the problem is the difficulty of selling to the United States. Even before the second World War there was a tendency for the United States to sell more than it purchased from the rest of the world. This was due partly to the rapid progress of technology in the United States, and partly to our tariff policy. At any rate, between 1870 and the latter twenties, manufacturing capacity in the United States grew from less than one fourth of the world's capacity to over 40 per cent.[4] Today the United States possesses about one half of the world's manufacturing capacity. Between the seventies and the last war, imports of manufactured goods into the United States dropped from about 38 per cent of all imports to less than one

[4] League of Nations, *Industrialization and World Trade*, II, A–10, p. 13.

fourth. Manufactured exports grew from one seventh of all exports to about one half.[5] The difficulties experienced by other countries in selling to the United States have been greatly aggravated by the war. In the year 1947 the United States sold $19.6 billion of goods and services to the rest of the world, and it bought $8.3 billion of goods and services. This meant that there was a deficiency of $11.3 billion to be made up. Such a huge deficiency cannot long continue. In the long run only a small part of exports from the United States can be financed by gifts. A substantial excess of exports can be financed by investments, provided the credit position of other countries improves. Their credit position, however, depends upon their ability to sell directly or indirectly to the United States. All of this means that in the next four or five years this country must either substantially reduce its exports or make a large increase in its imports.

It is essential to realize the crucial importance of a great increase in imports to the United States. Indeed, unless there is such an increase, the European Recovery Program will fail of its essential objective. It will increase the productive capacity of some European countries without making these countries really self-supporting. Let us assume, however, that the United States were able to increase its imports of goods and services to 7.5 per cent or 10 per cent of its national income. This would be somewhat above

[5] N. S. Buchanan and F. A. Lutz, *Rebuilding the World Economy,* p. 5.

the prewar period, when imports were running slightly more than 5 per cent of the national income.[6] By the end of 1951 the national income of the United States will be well above $225 billion a year in terms of 1947 dollars. If the imports of this country were from 7.5 per cent to 10 per cent of the national income, the United States would be creating annually from $17 billion to $22.5 billion of dollar exchange.

The mere provision of more dollar exchange would tend to increase the demand on the part of other countries for goods from the United States. Indeed, the improvement in the credit standing of other countries resulting from better opportunities to sell to this country might enable them to buy goods from this country with borrowed money. Hence, one cannot predict that even imports of roughly $17 billion to $22.5 billion a year into the United States would balance exports from this country. This volume of imports would, however, solve the problem of pay-

[6] In the three-year period 1936–8, imports averaged about $3.6 billion a year, or 5.2 per cent of national income.

National income is the aggregate earnings of labor and property which arise from the current production of goods. Hence it is usually less than the national product, which is the market value of the net output of goods and services produced by the economy. National product is higher than national income by the amount of business taxes and business transfer payments and less by the amount of subsidies. In 1947 the national income was $202.6 billion and the net national product $217.4 billion. In this chapter I have used figures for the national income rather than the national product (as in Chapter III) because figures for foreign countries with which comparisons are made are in terms of national income.

ing for exports, and save other countries from the possible necessity of reducing their purchases from this country, and hence of cutting either their consumption or the increase in their plant and equipment. A large increase in imports into the United States would greatly reduce the net cost of European relief and recovery to the United States. Indeed, if the increase in imports were large enough, there would be no net cost to the United States — this country would obtain goods equal in value to the goods it provided for Europe. I have emphasized the speculative nature of the European Recovery Program and the possibility that it might fail to achieve its objectives. The very fact that the program represents a gamble for the United States is a special reason for reducing the cost of it to this country to a minimum.

IV

Can the United States increase its imports of goods and services within the next four or five years to 7.5 per cent or 10 per cent of the national income? The percentage is only moderately above the prewar ratio of imports to national income. It is no higher than the ratio of imports to the national income one hundred years ago. At that time the United States was obtaining about 10 per cent of its standard of living by foreign trade. It is lower than the ratio of imports to the national income in most other countries. For example, in 1937, imports of merchandise only into

141

Sweden were 20 per cent of the national income; into Britain, Canada, and New Zealand, about 25 per cent; into Belgium, about 40 per cent; and into Norway, about 60 per cent. Nevertheless, increasing imports into the United States to 7.5 per cent or 10 per cent of the national income will be difficult in the extreme. In absolute terms this means an increase of $9 billion to $14.5 billion a year in imports at present prices. Let us put the increase needed at roughly $10 billion a year. There are several obstacles to achieving it.

1. The United States is a large country with a wide variety of resources and climates. It possesses rich stores of most basic raw materials, such as coal, iron ore, oil, other minerals, and timber; and its agriculture can produce economically most commodities that grow in temperate or semitropical regions.

2. The technology of American industries is superior to that of other countries. This superior technology is partly the result of the large domestic market of the United States. Hence in many industries other countries will be unable to adopt the methods of production that are economical in this country.

3. The expenditures on research, as I have pointed out, are large and likely to grow rapidly in the immediate future.

Perhaps it will be impossible for the United States to increase its imports of commodities and services by $10 billion a year within the next four or five years. In some cases purchases of equipment from the

United States are needed to enable another country to expand its sales to this country. A rise of even less than $10 billion a year in imports into the United States within five years will be of great help, however, provided it is substantial and shows signs of growing. There are several reasons for believing that a considerable increase in imports into the United States is possible within five years and that within ten years imports of commodities and services can be raised to 10 per cent of the national income. The United States is likely to become considerably more dependent on other countries for raw materials. Although great reductions have been made in the tariff during the last ten or twelve years, there is room for substantial additional cuts. The powerful trade unions will rapidly push up money wages, and will prevent technological progress from reducing labor costs in the United States. Finally, Americans may be expected to travel abroad in far greater numbers than ever before. Let us examine these several possibilities of increasing imports into the United States.

1. The growing dependence of the United States upon foreign countries for raw materials. The United States, as I have pointed out, possesses about half of the manufacturing capacity of the world. Its output of finished manufactured goods, and hence its consumption of raw materials, is rapidly expanding. Industrial production, for example, in 1947 was substantially more than double the rate after the first World War, and more than three times the rate immediately prior

143

to the first World War. Although the declining rate of population increase will somewhat limit the rise in the consumption of raw materials, every improvement in machinery increases the capacity of industry to convert raw materials into finished goods. Hence technological progress increases the drain upon the country's reserves of raw materials. Obviously the supplies for the large and rapidly growing manufacturing industries of the United States must come to an increasing extent from abroad. For example, the output of steel in the United States is as large as that of all other countries combined. It is unreasonable to expect that the iron ore for half of the steel output of the world will be drawn indefinitely from the ore reserves of the United States. Heavy inroads have been made during the last generation upon the country's high-grade ore reserves. Before the war, imports of iron ore constituted less than 5 per cent of domestic production. Although the use of low-grade ores is bound to expand greatly, the country should plan to increase its imports substantially. Imports of roughly five times prewar would be a desirable goal. In addition to being advantageous to the United States, such increases in imports would be helpful to Chile, Canada, Cuba, Sweden, and Brazil.

Even more important are large increases above prewar in the imports of lead, copper, zinc, bauxite, and petroleum. The consumption of all of these materials is rapidly growing. For example, in the last forty years the consumption of lead by the United States has increased over twofold; of zinc, by threefold; of copper, by fourfold; of aluminum, by twenty-five-fold; and of petroleum, by tenfold. The United States uses as much lead, copper, and zinc as the rest of the world. The reserves of copper possessed by the United States have a life of less than forty years, even at the 1935–39 rate of consumption, which was far below the post-war rate. The reserves of zinc, lead, bauxite, and asbestos have an even shorter life. Additional reserves of these minerals will undoubtedly be discovered, but they are not likely to be large ones. Despite the fact that commercial reserves of lead and zinc are quite limited, imports before the war were only 25 per cent of domestic primary production in the case of lead, and 12 per cent in the case of zinc. The United States should plan to obtain at least half of its copper, lead, and zinc from abroad. Even stronger is the case for large increases in imports of petroleum and petroleum products, because the use of these products in automobiles, airplanes, trucks, tractors, oil burners, and Diesel locomotives, is growing rapidly. The United States uses almost twice as much petroleum as all other countries combined, though it possesses less than one third of the world's reserves. The United States should not continue indefinitely drawing on its oil reserves at twice the rate at which the rest of the world is using oil. It should plan to import at least half of its requirements. In the past the United States has been a large exporter of petroleum products, but in 1947 it was an importer on a moderate scale.

145

Lumber is not an exhaustible resource, but it is not quickly and easily replaced. The United States is consuming substantially more lumber each year than its forests produce. In the case of trees of saw-timber size consumption is more than 50 per cent greater than growth. One must not expect the high rate of lumber consumption in the United States to be met entirely from the country's forests. Here is another great opportunity to buy more from abroad. Imports of softwood lumber before the war were only about 3 per cent of domestic production, and of hardwood lumber, about 2 per cent. If imports of lumber (in physical volume) were raised tenfold above prewar, about $400 million a year in foreign exchange would be created for Canada, the Scandinavian countries, Nicaragua, Mexico, Cuba, Brazil, Peru, the Philippines, or other countries. From 70 to 80 per cent of American consumption of lumber would still be domestically supplied. The consumption of saw-timber trees from domestic sources would be brought down to approximately the amount supplied by the annual growth of domestic forests.

2. The possibility of increasing imports into the United States through the reduction of duties. During the latter half of the nineteenth century the tariff of the United States was slowly being pushed upward. This process continued during the early part of the twentieth century. Moderate reductions were made in the tariff by the Democrats in 1892 and in 1913, but the general trend was upward. At the same time

that the United States was raising its tariff, it was out-running other countries in technological progress. As a result of the ever rising tariff and the superior technological progress of the United States, imports into this country gradually became smaller and smaller, relative to the national income. So high did the tariff become by the beginning of the second World War that the imports of the United States consisted largely of raw materials that are not produced in this country and came in duty-free. Indeed, about 60 per cent of the country's imports shortly before the second World War were on the free list. The concessions made by the United States under the Hull Reciprocal Trade Agreements and at Geneva in 1947 are estimated to have reduced the general level of duties roughly to the level of the Underwood Tariff of 1913. On 37 per cent of dutiable imports, however, no changes in tariff rates had been made by 1945.[7] This means that there is still substantial room for reductions.

Although most raw materials come in free, there are a few that pay either duties or import-quota excise taxes.[8] Lead, zinc, petroleum, and wool are examples.

[7] N. S. Buchanan and F. A. Lutz, *Rebuilding the World Economy*, p. 246. In 1945, duties had been reduced by 50 per cent (the maximum permitted by the act of Congress authorizing the trade agreements), in respect to 42 per cent of dutiable imports by value.

[8] Copper was made subject to an import "excise" tax of four cents a pound in 1932. This tax has temporarily been suspended The tax on crude petroleum is also in the form of an import excise

It is particularly desirable that the duties and excise taxes on lead, zinc, and petroleum be repealed, because they encourage the exhaustion of domestic supplies of nonreplaceable resources. The amount of such domestic production that is desirable for purposes of national defense should be stimulated, if necessary, by subsidies rather than by import duties. The duties on raw wool also should be repealed. There have been some reductions in these duties since the Tariff Act of 1922 placed a duty of 31 cents a pound, scoured basis, on fine imported wool, and the Smoot-Hawley Act of 1930 raised this to 34 cents a pound. The general agreement on tariff and trade concluded at Geneva on October 30, 1947, cut this duty to $25\frac{1}{2}$ cents a pound effective January 1, 1948. The high duties on wool, however, have not prevented farmers and ranchers from leaving the sheep business, or at least cutting the size of their herds. About 60 per cent of all the income from sheep raised in the United States comes from the sale of lambs. At the beginning of 1948 the United States had the smallest number of stock sheep in eighty-one years — though the market value of sheep was the highest ever recorded. Woolen and worsted manufacturers prefer foreign wools, which made up about 70 per cent of mill consumption of wool in 1947, and which commanded a premium of about 11 cents a pound over comparable groups of domestic wool. The principal reason for the

tax. Under the trade agreements with Venezuela and Mexico, this tax has been reduced to a quarter of a cent a gallon.

decline in sheep raising has been the better prices obtainable for beef cattle, hogs, and other products competing for sheep. The wool tariff is ineffective in maintaining a noneconomic industry, and it gives the wool growers only a small subsidy in relation to the additional cost it imposes on buyers of wool clothing.[9]

The most promising prospect of increasing imports through reduction of tariffs is in the field of dutiable manufactured goods. Many of these duties have been virtually prohibitive. Cheese pays high duties, and imports before the war were only about 10 per cent of domestic production. The United States might plan to obtain one third of its cheese from abroad. This would help Canada, the Netherlands, France, Italy, Norway, and Argentina buy American-made goods. Duties on pottery and china are enormous, and only about one sixth of American consumption comes from abroad. Duties might well be reduced until this proportion was raised to one third. Cotton cloth, wool cloth, cotton wearing apparel, wool wearing apparel, all present important opportunities to increase imports. The duties on these commodities are still enormous, even after the substantial reductions that have been made in various trade agreements. Imports of cotton cloth before the war were less than one per cent of domestic production, and

[9] For more extended discussion of this matter, see C. D. Hyson, "Wool and the Public Interest," *Farm Policy Forum*, April 1948, pp. 1–6. The above discussion of the effects of the tariff on wool draws heavily on Mr. Hyson's article.

exports were larger than imports; imports of woolen cloth were about 2 per cent of domestic production; of woolen wearing apparel, about 2 per cent; and of cotton wearing apparel of various kinds, about 7 per cent. I suggest a tenfold increase (over prewar) in physical volume of imports of cotton and woolen cloth and of woolen wearing apparel, and a threefold increase in cotton wearing apparel. This would leave over three fourths of the market in the hands of domestic producers, and would supply various countries, especially Britain, with roughly $200 million additional exchange a year.

The possibility of increasing imports of many varieties of goods, particularly manufactured goods, is improved by the existence of a number of nation-wide distributive organizations, such as Sears Roebuck, Montgomery Ward, a number of variety chains, and some organizations of department stores that practice some measure of centralized buying. Even some of the nation-wide food chains might become distributors of a few foreign-made food products. Up to the present, large American retailers have done relatively little to develop foreign sources of supply. The tariff has been the principal obstacle, although by no means the only one. Difficulties in getting goods to meet the preferences of American customers, problems of quick delivery (and particularly repeat deliveries), and the fact that most large American retail enterprises have not been organized to buy abroad on a large scale, have all limited the development of foreign sources

150

of supply. Were the tariff no longer an obstacle, many large retailers would undoubtedly gradually develop arrangements for obtaining goods from other countries. Many articles of apparel, many small household goods, much glassware and chinaware, could undoubtedly be purchased abroad for no more than must be paid for American products.

Reductions in the American tariff would not only increase physical imports into the United States; they would also raise the proportion of the American market price going to foreigners. Especially if duties are kept high enough to permit American producers to supply about nine tenths of domestic demand, most of the effect of lower duties would be to raise prices received by foreigners — and thus to increase the volume of dollar exchange available to foreigners.

3. The effect of trade unions upon imports. I have pointed out several times that the United States has the most powerful labor movement in the world, and that the unions here are likely to push up wages faster than the engineers and managers are able to raise output per man-hour. This process, of course, may be halted by the opposition of recipients of pensions and owners of fixed-income securities who find the purchasing power of their incomes reduced through the rise in prices. For some time to come, at any rate, the unions are likely to have a more or less free hand in pushing up wages. Consequently, labor costs are likely to rise. It would not be surprising to see labor costs increase about 25 per cent during the

next decade. This rise in labor costs would, of course, be reflected in prices. Unless unions in other countries are as successful as unions in the United States in raising wages, the prices of most American goods will rise relative to prices in foreign countries. This would be equivalent to a reduction in the tariff of the United States, and would help this country increase its imports.[10]

4. Increase in foreign travel by Americans. One of the best prospects for larger purchases of foreign commodities and services by Americans is the increase in travel abroad by Americans. In 1929 Americans spent almost $500 million on foreign travel. The number of Americans who can afford to travel abroad has greatly increased. Although people in all income brackets go abroad, the persons who may be regarded

[10] It is conceivable but improbable that the rise in wages and prices in the United States relative to prices abroad would increase the excess of exports from the United States over imports, and thus would aggravate the economic problems of other countries. This could occur if the demand on the part of foreign countries for exports from the United States were sufficiently inelastic — that is, sufficiently unaffected by a rise in prices in the United States. The result could be an increase in expenditures by foreign countries for American goods. As a matter of fact, many of the exports of the United States are sold in competition with other countries. Hence the demand of foreign countries for the part of the supply coming from the United States is elastic, or at least inelastic only to a slight degree. Hence a rise in prices charged by the United States is not likely to increase greatly expenditures by foreigners for goods purchased here, and it may actually decrease those expenditures.

as the best prospects for foreign travel are those with incomes of $5,000 a year or higher. In 1946 the number of such persons was approximately 4.6 million, in comparison with about 2.1 million who had the equivalent purchasing power of about $3,500 a year or more before the war. Total real income after taxes in the United States is about 50 per cent above prewar. Expenditures of Americans on foreign travel may be expected to increase far faster than real incomes. Many millions of Americans who formerly did not have vacations with pay are now receiving them. Furthermore, travel by air makes it easy for Americans to take short vacations abroad. Before the second World War, foreign travel was confined to a very small part of the country's population. This will no longer be true. It will not be surprising to see Americans by 1951 spending five or six times as much for foreign travel as in 1929.

V

Will not an increase in imports mean fewer jobs for American workers, unemployment, loss of production, and a drop in the standard of living? Certainly many people believe that imports are bad for employment here, and that they should at all times be severely restricted. Quite naturally these persons ask: "If most other countries need to increase their exports, why are not larger exports also good for the

United States?" Should not this country, therefore, seek to increase its exports rather than its imports?

I have already pointed out that exports are not an end in themselves, but simply a means of acquiring imports. If exports do not pay for imports, a country would be better off not exporting at all, but consuming all of its own output.[11] There is no doubt that a reduction in duties might cause painful adjustments in some industries. The severity of the adjustments would depend upon how much and how rapidly the duty was reduced; whether or not the resources of the domestic industry could be easily shifted to other uses; whether or not a small reduction in the price of the goods produced a substantial increase in demand (in other words, whether the demand was elastic or inelastic) ; whether or not the demand for the goods was rapidly increasing; and upon how rapidly demand was increasing for the ouput of the economy as a whole. A large increase of imports would not be tolerated at a time when production and employment were decreasing in the United States. Hence as a practical matter, the adjustment of the American economy to the economies of the rest of the world requires high and expanding production and employment in this country. Fortunately the great backlog of demand accumulated during the war makes the immediate postwar period a peculiarly favorable time for reducing

11 Exports may be regarded as paying for imports even though the proceeds from exports are invested abroad. In that case, exports pay for future rather than present imports.

duties. It means that most industries have demand in excess of their capacity. Postwar demand will remain far above prewar in most industries. Hence a substantial reduction in most duties would still leave domestic suppliers with larger markets than they had before the war.

The hardships that reductions in the tariff would impose on some groups are small in comparison with the good the nation as a whole would gain from a large increase in imports. Time was when duties helped the United States attract men and capital. They are no longer needed to do this. In a disturbed and uncertain world, capital has been attempting for years to enter the United States in embarrassingly large amounts, and if the United States were to remove its barriers on immigration, it would be flooded with people.[12]

The creation of $17 billion to $22.5 billion of dollar exchange a year would have far-reaching effects of great benefit to both the United States and all countries participating in the world recovery program. Five of these effects are especially important:

1. It would save other countries from the necessity of reducing their purchases from the United States, and thus from the possibility that they might

[12] A few of the duties have perhaps changed the terms of trade in favor of the United States — though duties that are virtually prohibitive do not do this. The principal effect of duties has probably been to reduce the price American exporters have been able to obtain for their exports.

be compelled to make a more or less serious reduction in their standard of living at the expiration of the European Recovery Program in 1951.

2. It would stimulate the expansion of industry in other countries, and help these countries raise the productivity of labor. Large sales to the United States would enable other countries to buy industrial equipment on a far greater scale than ever before. The enlargement and improvement of plants would raise the productivity of labor, and this in turn would raise the demand for labor and cause wages to rise. Workers throughout the world would be able to buy many products that heretofore they had been unable to afford. The opening of the markets of the United States to the rest of the world would greatly improve the credit standing of other countries. Hence their ability to buy from the United States would not be limited by their sales to this country, or by the willingness of the government of this country to make loans of more or less doubtful quality. A sound foundation would be created for a substantial increase in private investment by the United States abroad.

3. The chronic shortage of dollar exchange would be effectively eliminated. Most countries would be relieved of the necessity of continuing exchange controls, the licensing of imports, and the conduct of trade through bilateral arrangements. One should not expect, of course, that the mere abundance of dollar exchange would automatically and quickly produce a world-wide disappearance of restrictions on trade.

Some countries are determined to develop certain industries and will have to impose severe restrictions on certain types of imports in order to permit these industries to survive. Nevertheless, the basic condition for relaxing trade restrictions is an abundance of dollar exchange. Until the rest of the world has easy access to the great market of the United States, no general removal of restrictions on trade can be expected.

4. Good will and friendship toward the United States would be fostered throughout the world, because sellers are particularly well disposed toward their customers. The United States would be by far the largest customer in the world — in fact, it would probably buy between one fourth and one third of the world's exports.

5. The standard of living in the United States would be substantially improved. The increase in the flow of imports into this country would give Americans more to consume. In addition, the increase in sales to this country and purchases from it would foster the concentration of labor and capital in the most productive industries here, and thus help to raise output per man-hour.

One final word should be said concerning the contribution of the United States to the recovery of production and trade throughout the world — namely that the success of the United States in attempting to rebuild the economies of the world will depend upon the avoidance of substantial fluctuations in production and employment here. Since the United States produces over one third of the world's goods and represents more than one third of all the markets of the world, economic fluctuations here are bound to have great reverberations throughout the world. Likewise, if the United States succeeds in keeping production and employment steady, it will spread stability throughout all of the economies of the world.

V

The Prospects of the American Economy

What are the long-run prospects of the American economy? Is the standard of living likely to continue to double about every forty years as it has done during the last century? Are the conditions that created rapid technological progress and a vigorous spirit of enterprise likely to persist? Or is it true, as many people fear, that the incentives which have spurred men to great economic achievements are being undermined, that the economy is losing its capacity to grow and change, and that the burst of progress which made the nineteenth century an age of unprecedented opportunity is petering out? From now on, must one expect per capita output and the standard of living to rise less rapidly than in the past?

What is the outlook for prices? Although there was virtually no net change in the general price level between the end of the Napoleonic Wars and the end of the second World War, the record of the last several

159

centuries seems to indicate that the long-run movement of prices is upward. Today the wholesale price
level in the United States is over three times as high
as it was two hundred years ago, and over twice as
high as it was a hundred years ago. Will the long-run
movement of prices continue to be upward?

Although the long-run movement of prices has
been upward, it has not been steady. In addition to
the short-term cyclical movements of prices, there
have been intermediate upward and downward movements, usually lasting about 20 to 30 years. In particular, great wars have often been followed by an extended decline in prices. For example, the Napoleonic
Wars (which included the War of 1812 between the
United States and Britain) were followed by a decline in the price level of the United States from an
index of 125 in 1814 (1926 — 100) to 56 in 1849.
The Civil War was followed by a drop in the general
index of wholesale prices from 132 in 1865 to 47 in
1896. The first World War was followed by a drop
from 154 in 1920 to 65 in 1932. Will the second
World War be followed by a decline in prices for
two or three decades, as were previous major wars?

I

Let us first look at the outlook for production. I
have pointed out that many people are pessimistic
over the prospects for the economy, and that these
pessimists fall into three principal groups: (1) those

who believe that investment opportunities are becoming exhausted; (2) those who believe that the internal developments in modern business are destroying the capacity of the economy to make changes; and (3) those who believe that changes in public policy and the rise of the labor movement are unfavorable to enterprise. The best way to judge the outlook for production is to notice how rapidly it has been growing in the past, and then to examine the principal conditions that may retard or accelerate the rise in output. In other words, after projecting past trends, let us examine, first the case for pessimism, and then the case for optimism. It is convenient to analyze output, past and prospective, in per capita terms.

Between 1869–79 and 1929, per capita output, expressed in terms of constant purchasing power, increased well over threefold, or at the rate of about 2 per cent a year.[1] If output per capita continues to increase at the same rate, it will rise from about $1,510 in 1947 to approximately $3,533 (in terms of 1947 dollars) in 1990. Possibly output per capita will increase faster than 2 per cent a year — perhaps as

[1] Economic progress cannot be satisfactorily measured over a long period of time, because it consists in large measure of the output of new things — radios, airplanes, electrical apparatus of all sorts, new drugs and chemicals — and improvements in the quality of the goods produced, rather than merely increases in the output of the same things. Nevertheless, it is convenient and useful to construct series of figures that purport to indicate the change in the national product over long periods of time — despite the fact that such figures greatly understate the rise in the national product because they fail to reflect the improvements in quality.

161

much as 3 per cent a year. In that event per capita income in 1990 will be about $5,376. For some time the rate of population growth has been dropping. About the year 1990 the population of the country is expected to reach a maximum. Estimates of this maximum differ, but if there is no net immigration, and if there is medium fertility, it will be about 166 million.[2] If the population is 166 million and output per capita is $3,533, the total national product will be about $585 billion; if output per capita is $5,376, the total national product will be about $892 billion.

Is it fantastic to suggest that per capita output will be somewhere between $3,000 and $5,000 by 1990, and the net national product somewhere between $550 billion and $900 billion? The lower figure, of course, is simply a projection of past trends, but the rise during the last hundred years was a rapid one — perhaps too rapid to continue indefinitely.[3]

II

Let us first examine the case for pessimism. What are the conditions that, in the opinion of many peo-

[2] This estimate is slightly higher than the census forecast. It assumes that the unexpectedly rapid rise in population during the last several years represents a permanent gain but not a continuing trend. I suspect that the census estimates of population trends will turn out to be far too low.

[3] Some economists believe that there is a tendency for the rate of increase in per capita output slowly to decrease. The evidence on this point, however, is inconclusive.

ple, justify the fear that the economy is losing its capacity to grow? Ten of these conditions seem to me to be particularly worthy of attention:

1.   The drop in the rate of population growth. The rate of population growth affects the rate of increase in per capita income because it affects the amount of enterprise in the community — that is, the willingness and the ability of the community to accumulate capital, and the willingness of investors to put money into risky ventures. The rapid growth of population, as much as one third in some early decades of the nineteenth century, fostered business confidence, encouraged experiments and innovations, and made the economy more dynamic, because it tended to protect business enterprises against mistakes in expanding plant or in introducing new articles. This protection against mistakes is diminishing in importance.

2.   The possible decline in the proportion of the population in the labor force. There has long been a tendency for the age of those entering industry to rise. In 1900, 63.5 per cent of the male population below twenty was in the labor force; in 1940, only 35.4 per cent. The number of students graduating from secondary schools increased, between 1900 and 1940, sixteen times as fast as the population; the number of persons graduating from colleges and professional schools, eight times as fast. The proportion of the male population of sixty-five or more in the labor force has dropped from 68.3 per cent in 1900 to 42.2 per cent in 1940. The increasing proportion of women

at work has thus far prevented the rising age of beginning work and the declining age of retirement from reducing the proportion of the population in the labor force. If the age of entering industry continues to rise, and the age of retirement continues to fall, however, the increasing proportion of women in the labor force may be insufficient to prevent the labor force from becoming a smaller part of the total population.

3. The continued drop in the hours of work. In 1840 or 1850 the customary working week was from sixty-six to seventy-two hours. Today the forty-hour week is the standard in most industries. As wages rise, employees demand a shorter and shorter working day.[4] The larger their incomes, the more time they wish for enjoying their incomes. One must expect the six-hour day to become well established before 1990. It may limit substantially the per capita output of commodities and services.

4. The growing scarcity of natural resources. The best of the country's natural resources have been developed. From now on, additional raw materials will be obtained only through considerably increased outlay of labor and capital. The declining accessibility of raw materials will tend to offset the gains in productivity from technological progress.

5. The decline in the spirit of enterprise and in

---

[4] They might demand a longer working day. The fact that they do not means that for most workers the demand for income in terms of time and effort is inelastic rather than elastic.

the willingness of business managers to take chances. In the nineteenth century, business enterprises were headed in large measure by the men who built them up and who owned a large part of them — by Carnegies, Rockefellers, Wanamakers, Hills, Armours, Fields, Westinghouses, Swifts, Cranes, Woolworths, Fords. These owner-operators were bold and ambitious economic adventurers, eager to expand their concerns and willing to take big chances to do it. They have been succeeded, it is said, by cautious professional managers who are unwilling to take the chances necessary to permit industry to utilize the potentialities of modern science. "The impelling faith of today," says Thurman Arnold, "is that investments must be secure. That faith makes modern industry incapable of supplying the goods to create order out of the economic chaos of Europe or of stimulating competitive development of industry in the outlying areas of our own country." [5] Some old-family enterprises, owned by the children or grandchildren of the founders, seem to be operated primarily to produce a maximum of current income. This means, in some cases, that adequate depreciation is not charged, and that, in any case, replacements are kept to a minimum so that the largest possible payments can be made to owners.

[5] Thurman Arnold, "Must 1929 Repeat Itself," *Harvard Business Review*, January, 1948, pp. 32–45. The above argument is based in large part upon Mr. Arnold's article. See also J. A. Schumpeter, *Capitalism, Socialism, and Democracy*, Chs. XII and XIV.

6. The growing number of customs and rules that impede experimentation and change. As industry grows older, rules and customs regulating its activities develop and become more and more compelling. Some of these regulations are more or less unwritten rules, such as the well-established customs in some trades that manufacturers must not deal directly with retailers. Others are rules of trade unions (such as rules governing methods of wage payment and jurisdictional rules), or rules of trade associations; and still others are laws regulating selling practices, methods of construction, and methods of doing business. These rules and customs are likely to block the innovator who wishes to experiment with new methods of production or marketing, or who wishes to organize the work in a new way or try out new systems of wage payment. There can be no doubt, for example, that the "full-crew" laws applying to railroads and the more or less standard pattern of compensation prescribed by the train-service unions have discouraged experimentation with new types of trains and train service. In the building trades, laws and customs have impeded experimentation with new materials and new methods of construction.

7. The make-work rules of unions. A new union usually has all it can do to establish satisfactory wages, hours, and grievance procedures. After these matters have been taken care of, it may turn to make-work rules. A few of the oldest unions, such as some in the printing trades and railroads, are conspicuous for

their make-work rules. Hence, as unions grow older, a considerable part of American industry may be covered by make-work rules of one kind or another. Other rules of unions indirectly have the effect of make-work rules. For example, when a seniority rule is combined with payment by the hour, informal limitations on output may substantially reduce production below reasonable amounts. The men may attempt to make work by this means, and the management is deprived of effective instruments for counteracting restriction of output. If make-work rules or practices become prevalent, they will substantially hold down the output of industry and the standard of living of the country.

8.   The possible decline in the rate of technological discovery. The industrial revolution has been going on for two centuries. Many people believe that the discoveries that open up the greatest possibilities for increasing output per man-hour have already been made, and that from now on, technological progress will produce slower and slower increase in output per man-hour.

9.   The shift in demand from commodities to services. The amusement industry, hotels, restaurants, doctors, and dentists are examples of producers of services. As incomes rise, the demand for services will grow faster than the demand for commodities. Most of the service industries are believed to use less machinery and equipment per dollar of output than do the industries that produce commodities, and are

probably less susceptible to transformation by technological progress. The larger the service industries, the smaller will be the proportion of the labor force whose output will be affected by technological progress.

10.   Taxes and wage policies that impede the accumulation of capital. The basis for the large increase in production during the last two centuries has been in large part the great increase in the quantity of plant and equipment per worker. Of course, improvement in methods and in the quality of capital have also been important. Nevertheless, between 1880 and 1940, as I have pointed out, capital per worker trebled. An increase of roughly 2 per cent in capital per worker per year has been sufficient to make possible a rise of about 2 per cent in output per worker per year. The accumulation of capital depends (1) upon the ability of the community to save, and (2) upon its willingness to invest.

Both the ability of the community to save and its willingness to invest are being undermined, it is said, in various ways, but in particular by the strong upward pressure of trade unions on wages and by high taxes. The strong upward pressure of unions on wages is said to reduce both the ability and the incentive to accumulate capital. During periods of expansion there has usually been a lag between the rise of prices and the rise of wages. Trade unions may be expected to shorten this lag, thus reducing the profits of enterprises and the capacities of enterprises and their owners to save. In addition, the upward pressure of unions on wages is likely to raise wages relative to prices, and thus to raise the so-called "break-even" points of industries, that is, the rate of production at which costs are covered and profits begin to be made. The higher the break-even point, the less the incentive to expand capacity. An excellent illustration of the effect of high break-even points upon the expansion of capacity is furnished by the iron and steel industry. Between 1937 and 1947 the hourly earnings of steel workers increased by nearly 85 per cent, and the price of steel products by 35 per cent. Despite an increase of over 60 per cent in the tons of rolled steel, profits per dollar of sales dropped from 7.6 cents to 6.3 cents, indicating a substantial rise in the break-even point. There is a crying need for substantial additions to capacity in the steel industry. Since 1929, capacity has increased by only about 25 per cent, although manufacturing output for the country has increased about 75 per cent. With a high break-even point and a powerful union, steel companies are naturally reluctant to make the much-needed increase in steel capacity. Thus, the standard of living of the entire country is held down by the effect of high labor costs (and prospectively even higher labor costs) upon the willingness of the steel industry to expand.

The steeply progressive income tax greatly reduces the ability to save of the people who are best able to save, and who in the absence of high taxes would do most of the saving in the community. It also reduces the incentive to save, because for many well-to-do persons half or more of any increment of income gained from the investment of the saving would go to the government.[6] When the government takes such a large share of income, many investment opportunities that would otherwise be attractive cease to be so.

The trade-union movement will remain powerful and aggressive, and will undoubtedly become more so. Taxes must be expected to remain high for the indefinite future. From now on, the United States will need a large military establishment. This will require much equipment, and most of the equipment will have a short life. The military expenditures of the country are likely to be at least $15 billion a year, and may soon be as high as $20 billion. Pressure groups of various kinds — the aged, the farmers, the veterans, and others — are tapping the public treasury on a steadily increasing scale, and the politicians are becoming more and more aggressive in attempting to buy votes with public money. For these and

[6] Although there is no doubt that the high taxes reduce the ability of people to save, there is question as to whether they reduce the incentive to save. There is a good deal of evidence that men are willing to work longer hours for a low wage than for a high one. It is obvious, however, that this can be true only up to a certain point. If men are willing to work longer hours for a low wage, they may be willing to save more for a lower return after taxes than for a higher one. A tax of 100 per cent would obviously destroy the disposition to save. It is not known, however, at what point tax increases cease to stimulate saving and begin to discourage it. Taxes that take as much as half of any increment of income are probably fairly discouraging to most people.

other reasons the government's need for revenue will be great. There is little likelihood that the budget of the federal government will ever again be less than $40 billion, and budgets of $45 billion, or even $50 billion, are likely soon to become normal.

A feature of the personal income tax which is particularly unfavorable to progress is the special handicap it imposes on risky ventures. The effective tax rate rises with the degree of risk. It is not merely that the income tax is steeply progressive, because a progressive tax need not discourage risk taking. The difficulty results from failure of the tax to provide adequate offsets for losses. Consequently, the riskier the venture, the less attractive it is under present tax laws. All would-be investors have an incentive to put their money into the safest investment they can find.

The rapid progress of the last century was made possible largely by a buoyant spirit of adventure. There is no better way of destroying that spirit than by taxing risky investments at a higher rate than less risky ones. The present personal income tax may be expected to discourage particularly the starting of new enterprises, because new concerns are especially risky. Hence it tends to protect established concerns against the competition of new ones, and thus to make the economy less competitive and less dynamic. Of course, it would be easy to change the income-tax law, and this could be done without loss of revenue in the long run. In fact, in the long run the yield of the tax would probably be increased. The men of adventuresome and pioneering spirit, however, are too few to have much political influence. Furthermore, they are disturbing to many groups in the community. The heads of well-established business concerns fear them, and so do many trade unionists. Consequently, there is not much likelihood, in the view of many people, that the income-tax law will be modified to encourage adventuring.

III

The foregoing analysis paints a dark picture of the outlook for production. What is the case for optimism? It consists of three parts: In the first place, some of the reasons given for expecting a decline in the increase in output are open to question. In the second place, others are of minor importance. Finally, there are some conditions that will tend to cause output to grow even more rapidly in the future than in the past. What are the principal reasons for believing that the rise in output will be well sustained?

1. The rate of population growth will undoubtedly decline, but the labor force may become a larger instead of a smaller part of the population, especially if hours of work continue to be reduced as rapidly as in the past. Especially will the spread of the five-day week and the seven-hour and six-hour day attract a larger proportion of women into the labor force. The proportion of women in the labor force is still small (about one fourth of those over fourteen years

of age), and will undoubtedly continue to increase. The reduction in the work week will also tend to increase the number of young people who work while going to school — though the proportion of young people in the labor force will probably continue to decline for several decades. The assumption that the age of retirement will continue to decline is open to question. Thinking on the subject of retirement is undergoing great changes. It is now thought wise to encourage men to work as long as their health permits, and to protect them from being forced into retirement by employers. Managers may continue to press for early retirements, but the position of trade unions on the matter is changing. Hence the age of retirement may rise rather than decline. It would not be surprising to see the civilian labor force rise from its present proportion of about 56 per cent to nearly 60 per cent of the population [7] of fourteen years of age and over.

2. The hours of work will continue to decline, but probably not faster than in the past.

3. The United States will be compelled to use less accessible natural resources within its borders, but this handicap will be limited by the importation of raw materials from abroad. Many foreign

[7] The movement in and out of the labor force is very large. In 1947 the labor force varied from a low of 57.8 million in January to 62.7 million in July. The average number of persons in the civilian labor force was about 60.2 million. The number of persons who were members of the labor force at some time during the year was about 80 million.

sources of raw materials are quite as rich as those within this country. Hence the net disadvantage, if any, is likely to be little more than transportation cost.

4. The professional manager of the typical large enterprise of today is undoubtedly less inclined than the owner-operators of yesterday to take long chances, but his caution is offset in large measure by staff work. Indeed, the rise of staff work is one of the most conspicuous developments in business during the last generation. The fact that plans for improvements and expansion are not executed until much staff work has been done does not mean that managements lack enterprise or are unwilling to spend money on improving and expanding plant and equipment. The record of 1946 and 1947 refutes the assertion that managements are afraid of expanding production — for in each of these years substantially more than half of profits was reinvested in industry.

5. The customs of industry, and rules and laws that regulate its practices, may handicap pioneers and impede change, but one should not exaggerate the importance of their effects. The make-work rules of unions are a case in point. If employers do a reasonably good job of bargaining, these rules are not likely to become so widespread as to reduce materially the national product. In the first place, many unions obtain no advantage from limiting output. In the second place, the unemployment that some unions endeavor to prevent by make-work rules is usually

transitional unemployment that is associated with the introduction of labor-saving changes. Employers should be able to convince unions that this type of unemployment can be better met by temporary arrangements than by make-work rules of more or less indefinite duration. Unions themselves, as they gain experience, are likely to see that make-work rules frequently limit their ability to gain other concessions from employers. Far more important than make-work rules are likely to be arrangements by which unions and management co-operate to increase output and to reduce costs. Hence the net effect of unions upon shop practices may be favorable rather than unfavorable to production.

6. The belief that the rate of technological change is slowing down is likely to prove erroneous if one measures technological change by the over-all rate of increase in output per man-hour. Indeed, the industrial revolution now appears to be still in its infancy. Thus far man has manipulated matter in the main by rearranging molecules; now he is learning how to manipulate atoms. This will enormously advance his control over matter. The development of atomic power is likely to be quite as revolutionary as the development of steam, electricity, or internal combustion. Expenditures on industrial research have been growing rapidly for some time, and are likely to continue to grow. As I have pointed out above, if one enterprise spends money on research, its competitors must do the same thing or be left behind. The

strong upward pressure of unions on wages will encourage research. The support of research by the government is also growing rapidly, and will continue to
grow. Indeed within the last decade the government
has become by far the largest supporter of research in
the physical sciences. The interest of the government
in research stems in large part from keen military
competition between the United States and Russia.
Consequently, many discoveries will remain military
secrets; but much of the work sponsored by the government will have industrial applications.

7. As incomes rise, the demand for services will
undoubtedly increase faster than the demand for commodities, but the assertion that service industries are
less susceptible to technological progress than other
industries should be accepted with reservations. This
is not true of all service industries. One of the most
important service industries is transportation. It is
one of the industries most likely to experience a growing demand for its output as incomes rise. It is also
an industry in which technological progress is peculiarly effective in raising output per man-hour. Even
in the case of some professions, such as medicine, den-
tistry, and engineering, technological progress is important in raising output per man-hour, and also in
improving the quality of the service. A leading physi-
cian estimates that improvements in drugs and methods of treatment enable a doctor today to take care
of half again as many patients as twenty years ago.

Before that, the telephone and the automobile greatly increased the number of patients whom a doctor could efficiently serve.[8]

8. The personal income tax will undoubtedly remain high and steeply progressive, and the labor movement will be even more powerful than it is today, and possibly more aggressive; but these prospects do not mean that a substantial increase in capital will be prevented. I have pointed out that personal savings have not been a major source of venture capital, at least for the corporate part of industry. Nor should one assume that even a laboristic society cannot be

[8] The contrast of productivity in two groups of industries that correspond roughly to commodity producing and service producing is indicated by estimates of Hagen and Kirkpatrick for the period 1923–40. In a group of industries consisting of manufacturing, mining, transportation, electric-power and gas utilities, and construction, output per man-hour increased 77.7 per cent between 1923 and 1940. In the second group, consisting of wholesale and retail trade, communication, finance, and personal and professional services, annual output per worker increased 22.3 per cent between the same dates. "National Output at Full Employment," *American Economic Review*, September 1944, Vol. XXXIV, pp. 477, 478, 484, and 486. The latter figure fails to take account of change in the number of hours worked per year. Undoubtedly there was some drop, though it was probably less than in the case of the first group of industries. The reason is that the self-employed, who are more numerous in the second group than in the first, are less inclined than employees to reduce their hours. If the drop in hours were one sixth, the rise in output per man-hour could be 47.5 per cent.

The first group of industries includes one industry of the service category, classified by Colin Clark as among "tertiary industries" — namely transportation.

persuaded to make many reforms in the income tax in order to stimulate enterprise. For example, men may be encouraged to save and invest by being permitted to claim a special rebate on the proportion of incomes saved.

The corporate income tax, as well as the personal, will remain high. Most of this tax, however, is undoubtedly passed on in the long run either to customers or to wage earners. Consequently, stiff corporate income taxes do not greatly limit the capacity of most corporations to supply themselves with capital. Even a laboristic community may be willing to encourage investment by permitting business concerns to charge off new equipment in a relatively short period of time (say five or seven years) or to claim a rebate, as suggested in Chapter III, on the corporate income tax in the event that all of the depreciation allowance has been reinvested over a five-year period and no less than a given proportion of it in any year in the period.

The effect of high and progressive taxes and of strong upward pressure of unions on wages is likely to be offset in large measure by the use of inflationary methods of financing the purchase of plant and equipment — particularly equipment. In recent years the banks have entered the field of equipment financing to an increasing extent through the development of term loans. This type of loan is susceptible to much broader development. It is particularly desirable for firms that are too small to make public issues of stocks

178

or bonds. At any rate, so long as business concerns are eager to buy equipment, they may be expected to find ways of financing it.

IV

Which case is more persuasive — the case for pessimism or the case for optimism? With considerable assurance one may assert that the development of technology during the next generation or two will be a more powerful influence for economic progress than ever before. The two principal reasons for doubting the optimistic case are (1) the possibility that the community will be unwilling to reform the tax laws so as to avoid imposing stiff penalties on enterprise, and (2) the possibility that the strong and aggressive trade-union movement and public hostility to price increases will prevent adequate expansion of certain key industries.

Failure of the community to reform its tax laws may not be too serious a handicap for industry since, as I have indicated above, expansion can be financed (as it has been) in large measure by plowing back earnings and by borrowing from banks — particularly in the form of term loans. Hence the unfavorable effect of taxes upon the ability and willingness of individuals to save may not seriously impede the growth of industry. Far more serious is the danger that the output of all industry will be held back by high "break-even" points in certain key industries. Any *over-all* tendency for labor costs to rise faster than prices can undoubtedly be corrected, if necessary, by the fiscal policy of the government. A public policy of encouraging a slow rise in prices, however, would not assure that no industries would be squeezed between advancing wages and public resistance to price increases. The present condition of the steel industry is in point. There is no doubt that output in many industries is being held back by lack of steel. Indeed if steel were available in adequate amounts, the index of industrial production would undoubtedly be running above 200 instead of between 190 and 195. This would be possible with the present volume of employment. The existence of a strong trade union in the steel industry, plus the reluctance of the managements of steel companies to incur public disapproval by raising prices of steel, virtually assures that the break-even point in the steel industry will remain so high that new enterprises are not attracted into the industry and that existing concerns do not adequately increase their capacity.

If high break-even points prevent for many years adequate expansion of the steel industry or other industries producing raw materials used in making capital goods, the long-run rise in the output of the American economy will not justify the hopes of the optimists.[9] There are several ways, however, in which

9 Unduly high break-even points in scattered consumer-goods industries would be unfortunate but not particularly serious. They would prevent consumers from obtaining the most desirable mix-

the problem of too high break-even points in key industries might be met. One is development of the practice of paying more attention to break-even points in wage negotiations. Another is development of better appreciation by the public that high break-even points justify price increases in industries that need to expand. Another is importation of goods that are in short supply because of high production costs in this country. Canada, for example, might develop a low-cost steel industry to supply part of the American market. Still another is the building of capacity (such as steel capacity) by important users of the scarce product. Finally, the problem may be met in part at least by inventions that increase the output of present plant and equipment with little additional investment.

V

What is the outlook for prices? Although the index of wholesale prices at the present time is twice as high as it was a hundred years ago, virtually all of this rise has occurred during the last eight years. At the present time is the country to be regarded as standing at one of these temporary postwar price peaks?

Economists appear to be divided on the outlook for prices, but the preponderant opinion seems to be that the movement during the next decade or two will be downward. Among sixty-two nongovernmental econ-

---

ture of products from industry, but would not substantially reduce the standard of living of the community.

omists polled in 1945 by an agency of the Farm Credit Administration, the composite estimate was that the price level in the quinquennial 1956–60 would be slightly below the period of 1946–50. This group of economists, however, failed fairly completely to see the rise of more than 50 per cent in wholesale prices which has occurred since 1945. In fact, they estimated that wholesale prices for the quinquennial 1946–50 would be only 6 per cent above 1945. Since prices have risen much more than these economists anticipated, perhaps the subsequent fall will be greater than they predicted.[10] The economic experts for the Committee of European Economic Co-operation also seem to expect a decline in prices — at least for goods produced outside of Europe. In forecasting the balance of trade after 1948, these experts assume that the prices of imports into Europe in 1949 will be 7.5 per cent below the level of 1947; in 1950, 10 per cent below; and in 1951, 12.5 per cent below. Finally,

---

10 Although 62 economists gave forecasts for prices in the period 1956–60, a total of 144 were solicited for opinions, and considerably more than 62 expressed judgments concerning the postwar course of prices. For example, 21 expressed the belief that the price level will rise consistently over a considerable period of years; 14, that it will follow a level trend after the conclusion of a preliminary postwar rise; 43, that there will be a more or less extended decline in prices beginning about 1948–50; 14, that there will be a fairly extended decline about 1948–50, with recovery after the early fifties; and 15, that there will be a falling trend of prices, both for immediate postwar years and for a longer period. The wide diversity of opinion among the "experts" indicates the difficulties of making satisfactory forecasts.

a study made by the Bureau of Agricultural Economics for the House Committee on Agriculture reaches the conclusion that during the decade 1955–65, consumer prices will average about 10 per cent below 1947, and wholesale prices, about 18 per cent below.[11]

If one were guided by experience after earlier important wars, such as the Napoleonic Wars, the Civil War, and the first World War, one would expect that the movement of the price level for fifteen to thirty years after the second World War would be downward.[12] I do not believe, however, that the price trends after great wars during the last hundred years furnish a reliable guide for judging the future long-term movement of prices. Two important new factors have arisen. One is the huge increase in government expenditures. The other is the rise of a powerful trade-union movement.

[11] Eightieth Congress, Second Session, Committee Print, *Long-Range Agricultural Policy*, pp. 17–21.

Three estimates of prices were made by the bureau — one that assumed "intermediate employment" at depression levels, a second that assumed "intermediate employment" at "average level," and one that assumed high employment. The above forecasts of prices are made on the assumption of "high employment," namely employment of 62 million out of a population of 158 million, and a labor force of 66 million. The bureau describes high employment as the condition "most likely" during the decade 1955–65. Ibid., p. 17.

[12] The four wars that occurred about the turn of the century (the Spanish-American War, the Boxer uprising in China, the Boer War, and the Russo-Japanese War) were not followed by a period of declining prices.

After previous wars the expenditures of the federal government soon dropped to less than 5 per cent of the national product. There is no likelihood that this will happen again. Indeed, the expenditures of the federal government seem virtually certain to remain close to 20 per cent of the national product. I have called attention to the fact that despite the low level of government expenditures relative to the national output, the federal budget during the last 156 years has shown a deficit in two years out of five. With expenditures far higher than at any time in the past, deficits in the future will occur even more frequently than in the past. They will help increase the money supply, and thus to keep up prices.

Trade unions, as I have pointed out in Chapter II, are likely to push up wages faster than the engineers and managers succeed in raising output per man-hour. Consequently the community will have to choose between a creeping increase in unemployment, a rise in prices, or the control of wages through the enforcement of a national wage policy. Eventually the country, as I have indicated in Chapter II, may choose to enforce a national wage policy on employers and trade unions. This decision, however, is not likely to be reached until people have had the experience of living for some time under slowly rising prices. In the meantime, however, the community will need to tolerate rising prices or perhaps even to foster price increases in order to limit unemployment. There will, of course, be much talk in favor of lower prices, but

184

not much is likely to be done for some years about the basic causes for rising prices.

The long-run movement of prices in the United States will be affected by the fact that such a rise will not make it difficult for the country to pay for much-needed imports. Many countries could not possibly tolerate wage and price movements that substantially interfered with their ability to export, and thus to import. The United States, however, has a large surplus of exports over imports — a surplus that is embarrassingly large both to this country and to other countries. Consequently, as other countries restore or increase their capacity to export, a rise in prices in the United States relative to prices in other countries will be urgently needed to restore balance among the economies of the world. Indeed, unless prices in the United States rise relative to prices in other countries, the chronic shortage of dollars is likely to plague the world for decades.

VI

How Good Is the American Economy?

How good are American economic institutions, and
by what tests should they be appraised? Do they stand
up well under various noneconomic as well as economic tests? Are they consistent with the democratic
philosophy? Are they likely to hold their own in competition with other economic and political institutions? Will they enable America to maintain a position of leadership in the sphere of economics, and,
even more important, in other fields as well? In short,
do American economic institutions provide a favorable environment for the building of a great civilization? Now that private enterprise is under strong and
persistent attack by Russia, it is especially important
that Americans have definite ideas concerning what
they expect of their economy, and that they observe
whether or not it meets their tests. Let us examine first
how well the economy meets certain economic tests,
and then some noneconomic ones.

How Good Is the American Economy?

What principal economic tests should the economy meet? It should be good at increasing output; it should give people reasonable security and abundant opportunities; it should adapt itself readily to new conditions; it should distribute its product fairly; it should maintain a fair balance between the interests of consumers and the interests of producers; it should distribute a reasonable amount of product on the basis of need; it should not permit incomes to be acquired in uneconomic ways. How well does the American economy meet these tests?

1. Is the economy good at increasing output per man-hour? The answer to this question is obviously yes. The success of the economy in raising output per man-hour, as I have pointed out, is due fundamentally to the large number of enterprises and to the fact that each operates in the main independently of the others, so that each is a center of initiative, and so that there is widespread rivalry among them.

2. Has the economy provided people with reasonable security and abundant opportunities? Arrangements are badly needed, as I have pointed out, to assure that the economy operates more steadily, and more adequate compensation needs to be provided for the unemployed. In a progressive and competitive economy, however, some jobs are always being destroyed by technological and market changes and some firms are being forced out of business. This in-

187

security needs to be compensated by opportunity — that is, by an increase in jobs and in business openings. Judged by this test, the record of the economy is excellent. Jobs have increased faster than population, and the economy has given people a more and more abundant choice of employers and occupations, a chance to advance, and a good opportunity to enter business for themselves. Let us look briefly at these matters. In 1870, for example, less than 44.4 per cent of the population of ten years of age or over was in the labor force. By 1900 the proportion was 50.2 per cent; by 1947, 51.6 per cent. About 1.5 million of the 3.8 million enterprises outside of agriculture regularly have employees. This gives workers a wide choice of employers, and the movement in and out of the labor force gives people a good chance to exercise this choice. The number of occupations is being constantly increased. The electric light and power industry, the electrical-equipment industry, the petroleum industry, the chemical industry, moving pictures, radio, the automobile industry, and the air-transport industry, have all brought with them a host of new occupations. As the number of industries continues to increase, the number of occupations will also grow. Some occupations, of course, are extinguished by technological change, but the main effect is to increase the number of occupations.

Technological progress, as I have pointed out in Chapter I, seems on the whole to increase the demand for skill, although instances where it has had the opposite effect are easy to cite. The demand for speed and precision, however, seems to be insatiable, and there is an underlying tendency to give the individual worker more and more apparatus to manage. These trends increase the demand for skill. The growing use of apparatus increases the importance of the occupations concerned with maintenance and repairs — skilled occupations that demand ability to detect the source of trouble and to make the kind of repair or adjustment needed to remove it.

Finally, new businesses are fairly easy to start. Although the ratio of self-employed to employees has been declining, over ten million out of a labor force of roughly sixty million have elected self-employment. The number of business concerns outside of agriculture has more than doubled since the beginning of the century. Furthermore, it has increased faster than population. In 1900 there were twenty-one firms for each thousand persons; in 1947, twenty-six firms per thousand persons.[1] Indeed, at the end of 1947 the number of enterprises outside of agriculture stood at an all-time high, 29 per cent above 1929, and about one third above the wartime low. About 200,000 business births (as distinguished from transfers of existing firms) occur in an average year. The high mortality among new concerns suggests that it may be too easy for poorly qualified people to go into business.

Excellent as has been the record of the American economy in providing opportunities, serious short-

[1] *Survey of Current Business,* May 1948, pp. 11 and 15.

comings remain to be corrected. There is a wide disparity of educational opportunities in different parts of the country. Furthermore, in all parts of the country educational opportunity is still unduly dependent upon income — although less so today than formerly, and less so in the United States than in almost any other country. Progress in providing educational opportunity is indicated by the fact that between 1890 and 1940 the number of high-school graduates increased about sixteen times as fast as the population. The country has also failed to give adequate employment and educational opportunities to Negroes. This is less a failure of economic institutions than of social attitudes. Encouraging progress has been made in recent years in reducing discrimination against Negroes, but much still remains to be done. Within business concerns the problem of promoting on the basis of merit is still far from solved — though some organizations have made much progress in developing regular lines of promotion and in making selection less dependent upon the judgment of any one person.

3. Does the economy adjust itself effectively to new conditions? On the whole, the answer to this question seems to be yes. Public policy, it is true, often moves slowly and timidly, avoiding issues until a large part of the community sees that a problem exists and demands action. This waiting for the people to insist on a public policy is inevitable in a democracy. Business concerns, however, do not have to wait for the public to demand action, and hence are usually quick

to adapt themselves to changes. Every one of the millions of enterprises is a point of contact between industry and the conditions under which industry operates, and each is able to act independently in determining how to meet a new condition. If a given type of raw material is becoming scarce, hundreds or thousands of concerns may experiment with substitutes. If a new machine or process becomes available, scores of enterprises are ready to try it out under different conditions. Many concerns are always ready to test the desire of customers for changes in the kind of goods offered to them.

The adaptations made by individuals and by business enterprises are, of course, motivated by self-interest, and are made without regard to their effect upon the community as a whole. Some of them call for corrective action by public policies. The failure of the economy to enforce more effectively the interests that all or most members of the community have in common is undoubtedly one of its major weaknesses. Most of the decisions of business managements, however, are in the public interest. They result in conserving scarce resources, increasing the efficiency of men and equipment, or adapting the product more closely to the preferences of customers. Consequently, the advantages of having adaptation occur in the main through the decisions of thousands of managements or millions of people outweigh the disadvantages. The method places at the disposal of the community much knowledge and interest that would be

191

lost if decision making were concentrated in a few
central planners.

4. Does the economy distribute its product widely
and fairly? There is considerable concentration of income. About 20 per cent of spending units receive 47
per cent of money income, and 30 per cent of the
spending units receive only 9 per cent of the money
income of the country.[2] Concentration of income,
however, does not necessarily mean that income is
unfairly divided. That depends upon one's concep-
tion of fairness. If one believes that income should be
distributed in accordance with the contribution of individuals or their property to output as measured in
competitive markets, one would expect a fair amount
of concentration — at least if human abilities are dis-

---

[2] *Federal Reserve Bulletin*, August 1947, p. 961. A spending
unit is defined as all persons living in the same dwelling and belonging to the same family who pool their incomes to meet their
major expenses.

Some spending units may receive virtually no income because
no members of the spending unit may be at work. This is true for
the large number of spending units in which the former wage
earner has retired.

A family may contain more than one spending unit, as in the
case of a family with a person living in the household who does not
pool his income with the rest of the family. It is estimated that at
the beginning of 1947 there were roughly 46.3 million spending
units and 40.6 million family units. At that time there were about
34 million dwelling units occupied by families which represented
only one spending unit. In approximately 5 million dwelling units,
the families consisted of two or more spending units. *Federal Reserve Bulletin*, July 1947, p. 791.

tributed more or less in accordance with a normal distribution curve.[3]

I shall not discuss different concepts of fairness in distribution. Some people believe that incomes should be based upon contributions to production; others believe that incomes should be based upon need; still others believe that fairness consists of a compromise between distribution in accordance with productivity and distribution in accordance with need. Probably most persons accept this third criterion of fairness, but they differ with respect to how productivity should be measured, and also with respect to how far incomes should be based upon need. I wish simply to call attention to a few facts concerning the distribution of income — facts that the reader may find useful in judging the fairness of distribution.

One significant fact is the relationship between

[3] Responsibility for results seems invariably to be concentrated. In fact, this is one of the uniformities which may be called a social law. No matter what events or type of behavior one observes, one finds that relatively few people are responsible for a large part of the results. A few repeaters write most of the letters to the newspapers, a small part of the labor force in any plant causes most of the turnover. Likewise, the responsibility for accidents, absenteeism, or grievances is concentrated in a small part of the labor force — not, of course, the same minority in each case. If a suggestion system is installed, about one tenth of the employees will make about half of the suggestions. About 9 per cent of all farms with about 12 per cent of the farm population produce about 46 per cent of the agricultural output. The concentration of income appears to be less than the concentration of the results of most human activities.

changes in wages and changes in average output per man-hour. During the last several generations, earnings of workers per hour seem to have more than kept pace with the rise in output per man-hour. In 1940, hourly earnings of nonagricultural workers were about eight times as high as in 1840. Physical output per man-hour was about six times as high. The index of wholesale prices shows a rise of about 10 per cent, but, as I have indicated elsewhere, this index has an upward bias. The real price level in 1940 was slightly below the price level of 1840. It is plain, however, that the wages of employees have fully kept pace with the rise in average output per man-hour.

A second significant fact that bears on the fairness of distribution is the proportion of income going to property. In the first chapter I pointed out that capital per worker has been rising, but that the share of the national income going to property has been dropping — in 1940, reproducible wealth per worker was about three times as large as in 1880, but the share of income going to property had dropped from more than one fourth in 1880 to about one fifth in 1940. In 1947 it was about one sixth. These figures may suggest that property owners are not receiving a fair share of the national income. The mere fact that the share of property has dropped as capital per worker has gone up does not, however, prove that property owners are being unfairly treated — even if one accepts the proposition that incomes should be determined in the main by contribution to production. As capital per worker increases, the drop in the marginal contribution of property to production may prevent an increase in capital per worker from increasing the proportion of output going to capital. The figures do indicate, however, that there is no basis for the oft-expressed fears that incomes are becoming concentrated in the hands of property owners.

A third significant fact that bears on the fairness of the distribution of income is the shift during recent years in favor of the low-income recipients. This shift, of course, does not prove that income is more fairly distributed today — possibly the low-income recipients have gained unfairly. Between 1941 and 1946, however, the average real income of the lowest fifth of the families increased by 68 per cent; of the next lowest fifth, by 59 per cent; and of the highest fifth, by 20 per cent.[4] Between 1935–6 and 1946, the proportion of all income going to the highest fifth of the families dropped from 53.2 per cent to 46.8 per cent.

Two serious inequities in the distribution of income are inadequate compensation for pioneering and risk taking and inadequate compensation for holders of fixed-income securities. Inadequate compensation of risk bearing and pioneering is a result of the sharply graduated surtax and the absence of sufficient offsets for losses. The recipients of fixed incomes have been badly treated in the last few years — as always happens when there is a war. Perhaps the buyers of bonds should be regarded as taking the risk that the

[4] *The Economic Report of the President,* January 1948, p. 18.

price level may rise. Possibly people who buy or accept pensions should be regarded as taking the same risk. The buyers of bonds in past years, however, could hardly be regarded as contemplating the possibility that the government would depress interest rates as severely as it has done. The drastic depressing of interest rates has been defended as a way of reducing the cost of the war. It did not reduce the real cost of the war — it simply meant that the government picked out a small part of the community — the owners of fixed-income securities — to pay a particularly large share of the cost.[5]

5. Does the economy provide a reasonable balance between the interests of consumers and the interests of producers? Producers and consumers, of course, are to a considerable extent the same people, but this does not mean that the interests of consumers and the interests of producers do not clash. As consumers, the people wish to obtain each article for a minimum expenditure of their incomes. As producers, they wish to work without too much fatigue under pleasant, safe, and sanitary conditions, they wish to work steadily, and they wish the largest possible compensation for their services or the largest possible return on their invested funds. The national product is maxi-

[5] For many investors the hardship was not great. The refunding operations induced by the government's policy of reducing interest rates gave the owners of called bonds an opportunity to invest in equities if they desired. The option was not open to insurance companies. Nor was the option completely open as a practical matter to the trustees of many endowment funds.

196

mized when there is a proper balance between people's interests as consumers and their interests as producers. Neither consumers nor producers are content to let uncontrolled markets determine the way in which budgets and costs fall upon consumers and producers. Both groups sponsor laws and public policies intended to modify the results that markets produce.

In the nineteenth century, employment policies and conditions of work were determined pretty largely in favor of consumers — undoubtedly too much so. Men were hired only when their services were immediately needed, and dropped when the need disappeared. Consumers also obtained goods without paying a sufficient amount in many cases to make possible safe, sanitary, and pleasant working conditions. In the matter of wages, however, employees fared much better. As I pointed out in Chapter I, the effect of technological progress was primarily to raise money wages rather than reduce the prices of goods. Hence most of the gains of technological progress went to people in their capacity as employees rather than in their capacity as consumers. The tariff is an example of another area in which the interests of producers dominated public policy. So high were tariffs on many products that virtually no foreign-made goods came in to compete with the domestic products.

Today the interests of producers seem in general to be more effectively protected than the interests of consumers. It is true that there are important respects

in which protection has been given to consumers —
the pure food and drug acts, legislation regulating
the issuance of securities and dealing in securities,
regulation of the maximum charges of railroads and
public utilities. Likewise, the position of consumers
has been greatly improved by the rise of chain stores,
mail-order houses, and department stores, which have
given consumers abler and more powerful purchasing
agents than they have ever possessed. On the whole,
however, the developments of the last several generations seem to have been mainly in favor of producers.
Many states have passed laws authorizing a manufac-
turer to fix the prices that retailers charge for his
product. Much legislation has been passed in the special interest of employees. The rise of powerful trade
unions has greatly strengthened the position of employees. It looks as if wages would be fixed primarily
in the interest of employees, and that wage policies
will require, as I have pointed out, a slow rise in the
price level. One producer group for which little con-
sideration has been shown, however, are the owners
of business enterprises and the providers of investment-seeking funds.

6.   Does the economy distribute enough income on
the basis of need? How much is "enough"? In 1946,
social-insurance benefits, old-age assistance, workmen's
compensation payments, public relief, and various
other payments based on need such as private pensions and fellowships (exclusive of mustering-out payments to soldiers) were about $9.5 billion, or 5.3 per

cent of all personal incomes.[6] These payments were about 70 per cent more than the total dividend payments of all American corporations, and nearly 22 per cent more than all corporate profits after adjustment for inventory gains. In Oklahoma more than half of the persons of sixty-five years or more receive old-age assistance, and in several other states old-age assistance is given to more than four out of ten persons of sixty-five or more. During the last twenty years there has been a rapid rise in incomes distributed on the basis of need. In 1929, payments under workmen's compensation plans, old-age pension plans, old-age assistance, and unemployment compensation were about $1.3 billion, or 1.5 per cent of personal incomes; and in 1940, about $3.1 billion, or 3.9 per cent of all personal incomes.

In addition to cash incomes based upon need, the government provides many free services, such as free primary and secondary education, fire protection, police protection, and the free use of many public facilities, such as parks, roads, and bridges. In fact, nearly all of the services provided by the government, which

[6] Some of these payments, such as pension payments, unemployment compensation, and compensation for industrial accidents, may be regarded as a part of wages. Certainly they affect the wage rates that are needed in different occupations and industries in order to attract and hold workers. Nevertheless, these payments come into effect when a need for them originates. Consequently, they are properly listed under income distributed on the basis of need — though to the extent that they are supplements to wages, they also represent income distributed on the basis of productivity.

are about one eighth of the total output of the country, are free to the particular individuals who use these services — although the cost of providing them falls upon the community.

Despite the great increase in incomes based upon need, much still remains to be done to protect people against want. For example, the federal old-age pension law applies to only about three out of five jobs. The self-employed, agricultural employees, domestic-service employees, and employees of nonprofit institutions are excluded. The coverage of unemployment compensation and workmen's compensation is likewise incomplete, and the compensation paid is usually too small. One of the most serious lacks is the absence of insurance against total disability for long-extended duration. On any day about 2 million persons are kept from gainful work by disabilities that have continued for more than six months. Although most workers now have old-age pensions and life insurance, protection against loss of income from total disability is not generally available. Another serious lack is the absence of free medical service and the absence of cash sickness and disability benefits. It is obviously preposterous that any one should fail to obtain medical service because he is unable to pay for it, or that he should have to receive medical service as charity rather than as a matter of right.

7. Does the economy permit a substantial amount of income to be acquired in uneconomic ways — that is, by misrepresenting goods, by restricting produc-

tion, by shifting real costs of production to workers or to the community, or by wasting resources? No reliable estimate of the amount of income acquired in uneconomic ways is available. The difficulties of making such an estimate are perhaps insuperable because many incomes are acquired by a mixture of economic and uneconomic ways — as when an article is represented to be better than it is. Perhaps someone will attempt to make rough estimates of the size of the principal forms of uneconomic incomes. An annual estimate, with a classification of the particular types of uneconomic income, would spur the community to eliminate these forms of income.

Considerable progress has been made in recent years in reducing the opportunities to earn a living in uneconomic ways — particularly by misrepresenting goods or unfairly shifting costs. Pure food and drug acts, the securities and exchange act, the introduction of standard grades, are all examples of the attack upon misrepresentation. Workmen's compensation laws and zoning ordinances illustrate efforts to prevent the unfair shifting of costs. Possibly some progress has been made also in discouraging the growth of monopolies. Certainly the laws against combinations are enforced more vigorously than in the past. The vigor of competition, however, depends largely upon the rate at which industry is attempting to expand. Tax laws, which make risky ventures less attractive relative to safe ventures, probably reduce the vigor of competition more than do all of the efforts of businessmen to create understandings and combinations. Likewise, rapid technological progress has probably done more than the anti-trust laws to keep competition keen.

Men will always be inventing uneconomic ways of making a living. Indeed it is part of the essence of private enterprise that men have great opportunities and great incentives to obtain incomes in new ways. Some of the new ways will add to the total national product; others will subtract from it. Consequently, the community must always be vigilant to prevent men from acquiring incomes in ways that reduce the net output of industry.

II

Does the economy meet the noneconomic tests that should be applied by a civilized community? Four tests are particularly important. In the first place, industry should be so operated as to respect human personality and to treat its workers as human beings rather than machines. In the second place, the conduct of industry should be favorable to the development of the noneconomic activities of the community. This means that it should be favorable to the development of ideas, experiments, and thinking in the arts and sciences — in literature, art, philosophy, science, and religion. In the third place, the economy should furnish a favorable environment for democratic institutions and processes. In the fourth place, economic institutions should help build a satisfactorily balanced scale of values — that is, a scale of values in which the interests that all members of the community have in common are ranked high in relation to the interests of individuals or of small groups. How satisfactorily does the American economy meet these four tests?

1. Is industry operated with proper regard for its workers and their needs as human beings? Are employees protected from arbitrary treatment by supervisors, and are they given a good chance to grow and to improve themselves? During the last generation there has been virtually a revolution in the managerial methods of many concerns, especially large ones, but much still remains to be done. Most large concerns have deprived foremen of arbitrary authority to make such decisions as who is to be promoted or laid off, or what discipline is to be imposed in a given case. The foremen simply make recommendations to a superior or to a personnel department. Shop rules have been instituted which give employees rights and which supervisors are expected to observe. A check on the treatment of employees by supervisors is sometimes made by "exit interviews" — interviews with all men who resign. The rise of trade unions has helped to spread better managerial practices, because unions introduce into industry arrangements by which the decisions of management may be challenged. Their influence is important even in many shops where employees are unorganized.

Developments of extreme significance are on the point of occurring in American management. Business heads are making systematic efforts to determine what employees think of their jobs, and what, in the employee's mind, are the elements of a "good job." Some managements, such as those in General Electric and Lever Brothers, are attempting to make every job in the enterprise satisfy the elements of a good job. They are arranging for each supervisor regularly to interview every employee under his direction, and for management to keep in touch with what employees think about their jobs and their supervisors. By and large, the outlook is bright in American industry for more understanding and humane treatment of employees than has ever occurred in the history of the world.

2. Are the economic institutions of the country favorable to the development of great work in noneconomic fields, such as art, literature, religion, science, and philosophy? Is artistic or intellectual life controlled in the interests of particular economic groups, is originality throttled, is the artist or thinker denied a fair opportunity to criticize the powers that be or to seek acceptance of new ideas, new conceptions of art? Artists, writers, philosophers, and editors could perhaps answer this question better than economists. Doubtless every one of them is impressed by the fact that the market makes demands on him which he does not like. Certainly the demand for trash is tremendous, and the temptation to cater to

it is great. It is also true, however, that the economic institutions of the United States are exceptionally favorable to competition in the field of ideas. They give sponsors of new ideas in the fields of art, philosophy, science, or religion an excellent chance to win converts or to find fault with prevailing ideas or established canons of taste. There are several reasons for this:

a.   The opportunity to pursue the arts while holding routine business or industrial jobs is good. The champion of a cause need not be too concerned over what his employer (if he has one) thinks of his ideas, because there are plenty of employers.

b.   There is no official censorship, no party line to be observed, no ideological tests to be met, no Zhdanov to lecture the artistic community on the state of its work, and no Central Committee publishing a *Culture and Life* for "the purpose of promoting criticism of deficiencies in ideological work."

c.   The fact that markets in the main are private means that the original thinker or creative worker is free to seek customers wherever he can find them. The customers may be individuals, municipalities, lodges, clubs, trade unions, churches, or corporations. Hence it is possible for men to make livings (and not infrequently good ones) by crusading for new ideas, by producing work that affronts accepted canons of taste, by publishing books and magazines of protest. Perhaps it is too easy to do these things. Undoubtedly the country would get better work if buyers were harder to please. These observations, however, are not criticisms of the economic institutions of the country. These institutions give workers in the arts a peculiarly favorable opportunity to produce free from control by the government, the church, business, or other established institutions, and to win support wherever they can find it. Americans may take pride in the fact that no community has ever given wider latitude to critics of its institutions than does the United States.

3. Does the economy furnish a favorable environment for democratic institutions? Many people believe that the thinking of the community is largely controlled on behalf of powerful economic interests, that political parties are simply the creatures of economic groups, and that the rise of powerful economic organizations has largely emptied democratic forms of their significance.[7] There can be no doubt that well-organized groups have influence in politics far out of proportion to their numbers — as is indicated by innumerable privileges, subsidies, and favors conferred on special groups. The fact that unorganized individuals frequently have scant attention paid to their interests is regrettable and may be regarded as a defect in democratic institutions. It does not mean, however, that these institutions have lost their significance or have failed rather completely. It does, of course, mean that democracy has the problem of

[7] This view is expressed by E. H. Carr in *Conditions of Peace*, p. 28.

maintaining a proper balance between the representation given to interests most members of the community have in common and that given to the interests of small groups. Although the influence of various small groups upon this or that aspect of public policy is considerable, there is no pronounced concentration of economic control — no dominant economic group that controls the government for its own purposes.

Two basic characteristics of private enterprise explain why it is favorable to democracy. One is that, under private enterprise, critics, dissenters, and rebels of all sorts do not find too great difficulty in making a living. The multitude of employers is helpful to the rebels. So also are the numerous opportunities for self-employment and the ease with which new enterprises can be started in many lines of business. Indeed, crusading for reform under private enterprise may be a good way of making a living. Certainly no other economic institutions offer the dissenter an equally good chance to support himself by crusading for change. Democracy would operate under a heavy handicap if organs of opinions and expression were all government-owned — if every newspaper, every magazine, every play, every book, every moving picture, and every radio program were produced by the government.

A second reason why private enterprise is favorable to democracy is that under it power is divided and widely dispersed. There are holders of great economic power, such as business leaders and trade-union leaders. There are also holders of great political power. Control of all production by the government would substitute concentration of power for the present wide dispersion of power. The present division of power between political leaders, industrial leaders, and labor leaders may be compared to the division of power between the Church and the State. The separation of the Church and State which has been characteristic of western Europe undoubtedly provided a favorable environment for the growth of the democratic philosophy. In eastern Europe, where the Church was subordinate to the State, there was no effective challenge to the extreme claims of the State. Hence people were led to continue to accept the idea that no one possessed rights against it.

Striking evidence that the American economy and political institutions are favorable to democracy is furnished by the rise of the labor movement. Trade unions were bitterly and vigorously opposed by employers, who were the dominant group in the community. Nevertheless, unions grew until today they are the most powerful economic organizations the country has ever had. The rise of trade unions in the face of strong opposition from employers is an encouraging fact. It should fortify the faith of Americans in their institutions, because it means that other shifts of power can probably be achieved gradually, peacefully, and in the face of strong opposition from established interests.

4. Do the economic institutions of America help

build a satisfactorily balanced scale of values? The scale of values of the community determines what importance is attached to purely individual interests, to group interests, and to the interests that virtually all members of the community have in common. No two persons will be in complete agreement concerning the relative importance that should be attached to various interests. Everyone will agree, however, that the scale of values the community accepts is of great practical importance. A community that attaches extreme importance to individual and group interests has great difficulty in developing policies designed to promote common interests. On the other hand, a community that attaches too great values to interests regarded as common may impose too complete conformity upon its members, and may limit its capacity to change and to adapt itself to new conditions.

Private enterprise may well cause men to attach more importance to individual and group interests than they would attach under some measure of socialism — though the controversies between the Coal Board and the employees in the British coal industry over installation of technological improvements and the division of the gains from them indicate that socialism does not prevent the growth of self-centered groups.[8] It is the essence of the socialist indictment of private enterprise, however, that too great scope is

[8] For some of the difficulties of the British coal industry, see the *Economist,* May 22, 1948, p. 826, and pp. 847–8.

allowed for the pursuit of private and group interests. The rapid growth of highly organized groups during the last several generations creates the danger that people will be trained to attach too great importance to group interests and will become narrow and parochial. Each person must reach his own conclusion as to whether or not he likes the kind of value judgments people are encouraged to make by the institutions of private enterprise. The danger that these judgments will be unduly narrow is real. The best protection against this danger is plenty of contact among persons from all manner of groups, good agencies of communication in the community, and a strong system of liberal education.

III

The American economy is a far better economy than most people realize. It is far more productive than most other economies; it is dynamic and progressive; it possesses great capacity to adapt itself to new conditions and to improve its methods and products; it has a multitude of points of contact with consumers, and does more than any other economy has ever done to discover the desires and whims of consumers; it is an economy in which there is broad participation in control, partly through democratic political processes, partly through millions of people who are in business for themselves and who run their own enterprises, and partly through the membership of millions of employees in trade unions.

The transformation of the American economy from a capitalistic to a laboristic society is occurring at a time when the United States has acquired a position of far greater economic importance in the world than any country has ever possessed. The transformation is also occurring at a time when the political and economic institutions of western Europe (and especially those of the United States) are being attacked through a carefully planned crusade organized by Russia. The object of this crusade is nothing less than the complete overthrow of Western institutions.

Will the new laboristic economy in the United States be able to give the world the kind of economic leadership it needs? Will it effectively stimulate growth of production? In particular, will it provide favorable conditions for innovators and pioneers? Will it keep production stable? Will it be able to champion effectively the institutions of freedom against the Russian efforts to destroy them? Will it be able to win new converts to freedom and eventually help the enslaved masses in Russia itself to win their freedom?

No one knows the answers to these questions. The new laboristic society will give other countries the kind of economic leadership they need provided it is good at increasing production and willing to increase imports. Although rapid technological progress in the

211

United States has created serious problems for some countries, a great rise in output in the United States will help other countries, provided the United States increases its purchases as rapidly as it increases its output. Furthermore, rapid economic progress in the United States reduces the danger of an attack by Russia, because it increases the potential military power of the United States.

Will the millions of employees who will be the most influential group in the laboristic society that is emerging appreciate their stake in a vigorous spirit of enterprise, in the rapid accumulation of capital, and in rapid technological progress? At present there is little evidence upon which to base either an optimistic or a pessimistic forecast. The ideas of employees are molded in large measure by trade unions, and the traditions of the trade-union movement in the United States are highly particularistic. Each union is pretty much concerned with its own affairs and its own problems, and feels little responsibility for the interests of labor as a whole. It is undoubtedly true, however, that employees as a whole have much to gain from effective policies for stimulating enterprise. The truth is powerful and one should not underrate its influence. Certainly it is at least probable that employees will discover their stake in enterprise and progress and that they will support public policies that foster enterprise.

In important respects the ability of the country to meet the challenge of Russia is improved by the shift of power from capital to employees. The participation of employees or their representatives in policy-making means that new problems are seen sooner and more clearly, and that policies are based upon more complete information and better understanding of conditions. Likewise the participation of employees or their representatives in policy-making forces them to abandon their position of side-line critics and to assume their share of the responsibility for decisions — including their share of the inevitable mistakes. This is a wholesome condition. A regimented economy in which individuals are vassals of the state will have more difficulty in commanding the allegiance and confidence of the people than does a laboristic economy in which responsibility for basic policies is widely dispersed.

The new laboristic society that is emerging in the United States has an opportunity to build far better economic institutions than the world has ever seen. It has a chance to keep the best features of capitalism — the large number of enterprises and the considerable decentralization of decision making which keep industry in close touch with conditions, which make it flexible and adaptable, and which have been responsible in large measure for the tremendous dynamic drive of the economy. It has an opportunity to improve greatly on the institutions of capitalism by broadening the objectives of business policies, by introducing civil rights into industry, and by greatly widening the participation of the community in making public policies. It should be able to develop ways and means of keeping industry operating steadily without large ups and downs. Possibly it will succeed in opening the markets of the United States to the rest of the world and in developing far closer economic ties between this country and other countries. If the new laboristic economy can achieve these results, the rate of industrial progress attained under capitalism will be maintained and the standard of living should continue to double every forty years or less.

Index

Index

Index

Index

iv

Index

Index

Index

A NOTE ON THE TYPE USED IN THIS BOOK

This book was set on the Linotype in a type-face called "Baskerville." The punches for this face were cut under the supervision of George W. Jones, the eminent English printer and the designer of Granjon and Estienne. Linotype Baskerville is a facsimile cutting from type cast from the original matrices of a face designed by John Baskerville, a writing-master of Birmingham, for his own private press. The original face was the forerunner of the "modern" group of type faces, known today as Scotch, Bodoni, etc. After his death in 1775, Baskerville's punches and matrices were sold in France and were used to produce the sumptuous Kehl edition of Voltaire's works.

This book was composed by The Plimpton Press, Norwood, Massachusetts, and printed and bound by H. Wolff, New York.

Date Due

FEB 3 '61			
OCT 19 1962			
	PRINTED IN U. S. A.		